Spooky Creepy
Long Island

Schiffer Publishing Ltd.®
4880 Lower Valley Road, Atglen, Pennsylvania 19310

Scott Lefebvre

Published by Schiffer Publishing Ltd.
4880 Lower Valley Road
Atglen, PA 19310
Phone: (610) 593-1777; Fax: (610) 593-2002
E-mail: Info@schifferbooks.com

For the largest selection of fine reference books on this and related subjects, please visit our web site atWe are always looking for people to write
books on new and related subjects. If you have an idea for a book please
contact us at the above address.

This book may be purchased from the publisher.
Include $3.95 for shipping.
Please try your bookstore first.
You may write for a free catalog.

In Europe, Schiffer books are distributed by
Bushwood Books
6 Marksbury Ave.
Kew Gardens
Surrey TW9 4JF England
Phone: 44 (0) 20 8392-8585; Fax: 44 (0) 20 8392-9876
E-mail: info@bushwoodbooks.co.uk
Website: www.bushwoodbooks.co.uk
Free postage in the U.K., Europe; air mail at cost.

Designed by "Sue"
Type set in Poornut/NewBskvll BT
ISBN: 978-0-7643-2814-5
Printed in China

Contents

Acknowledgements

Thanks and credit and favors owed:

Josh Gravel for more reasons than I can briefly summarize.

Rick Laprade and Corey Gomes for making me a supervillain.

Brian Harnois for being a great guy and comping me on the E.S.P. trip.

Ray Dowaliby from *SCARS* Magazine for giving me a reason to start writing again.

Nick Reid and Brian Dombrowski for being great roommates.

Tom D'Agostino for writing *Haunted Rhode Island*, returning my call, and answering all of my questions.

Dinah Roseberry from Schiffer Books for asking me if I could write and checking in on me regularly to remind me that I was writing a book for her.

Alyson Charlette and Dawn Roux for printing out and reading the draft I e-mailed them. Their suggestions and encouragement have been priceless.

Pete Bune from The Ghouligans for being receptive to my questions and putting me onto more than one of the right trails.

Keriann Flanagan Brosky and Linda Lee Macken for their generosity.

The miscellany of paranormal research and ghost hunting groups of Long Island for making their research readily available.

Anyone that made an offer of assistance or lent a word of encouragement.

And anyone reading this regardless of whether or not they bought a copy.

Meet Scott Lefebvre!
Or How This Book Got Made)

It all began as an accident.

I've been a fan of all things creepy and spooky for as long as I can remember.

It began with the horror anthologies of Helen Hoke and Alvin Schwartz.

Those few of you that haven't experienced the *Scary Stories to Tell in the Dark* books are only depriving yourselves. The storytelling and artwork are superlative.

As I got older, I moved out of the children's section and read everything there was to read about ghosts, witches, vampires, and monsters, back when you had to look up the subjects in the card catalog.

In the horror section of the library I found Stephen King and read every book of his the library had. I know many of you are rolling your eyes at the invocation of the "King" of horror, but when you're in fifth grade, reading about people doing terrible things to each other, the kind of things that your parents and your teachers never tell you about, well, it's scary enough. It's like there's a secret room at the shadowy end of the hallway of our collective unconscious and King was the first author to give me the key. Although his florid and profuse descriptive vocabulary are often the subject of derision, in fifth grade I was reading at the level of your average forty year old, and I think that the rich context and driving narrative of King was responsible for the credit or blame.

Then word got around about a guy by the name of Clive Barker who was reputed to write even more shockingly, frighteningly, horrifically, and to do so with an even greater intensity, so I read everything that blood-spattered Brit had available. The scars still swell on certain days, and I don't think I ever got all of the blood out of my dreams.

In school, they introduced me to Edgar Allan Poe, and although the author's black cats, tell-tale hearts, and gothic settings for stories about men in love with dead girls, were a welcome respite from the punishing discipline of laboring under the Western canon, few would say his work inspired fear.

They *gave* us Poe, but we were left to rediscover Lovecraft by ourselves.

Living in Providence, Rhode Island, the discovery was especially wonderfully nefarious because I could visit the places that he had written about. Everything was in walking distance and it added an additional dimension of reality to his tales.

That explains the paper trail.

There's still the trail of flesh and blood and word of mouth.

For the past few years I've been helping out with the Rhode Island International Horror Film Festival. I started as an attendee and soon became involved on the other side of the velvet ropes.

My friend, Josh Gravel, got involved before I did, and is probably mostly responsible for my continued involvement in both the film festival and all things horror. We've been friends since high school and we talk several times a week, hours at a time, about all things horror. Horror movies, horror books, and horror conventions.

I explain the preceding because somehow Josh got involved with a guy named Ray who was working on putting out a horror magazine under the title *Scars*.

Ray said he needed someone to review horror books and video games, and of course Josh thought of me, because outside of working and sleeping I mostly read books and play video games.

I jumped on the book review thing with both feet.

At the 2006 Rhode Island International Horror Film Festival, I met Thomas D'Agostino, the author of *Haunted Rhode Island*. I asked if I could have a copy of his book for review. Tom explained that if I wanted a free copy I could contact the publisher and he gave me a catalog.

I sent an e-mail to the publisher and asked for a copy of the book, and anything else they wanted reviewed. Dinah asked me if I wrote.

She thought I lived in Massachusetts and asked me if I lived too far away to write a book about supernatural happenings in Long Island. I replied that I lived in Rhode Island, but Long Island wasn't too far.

I accepted and planned on doing exhaustive research and cashing in some vacation time from work.

And that, I suppose, is how this book got written.

I put a great amount of time and effort into it and I tried to make it as comprehensive and entertaining as possible.

I hope you enjoy the results.

I look forward to hearing any thoughts you have about the book or its subject matter.

Feel free to drop me a line at Scott_Lefebvre@hotmail.com

I'll reply to your messages as time permits.

Introduction

Ghosts. Witches. Vampires.

Monsters that only come out by the light of the moon in remote and vacant places.

Old places.

Houses or buildings or places where people did evil or unfortunate things to themselves or others, or where they met their untimely end through misfortune or accident.

Places with memories.

Places that look like they should be haunted, even if they're not.

Places like old graveyards, abandoned churches, lighthouses and mental hospitals.

These are the birthplaces of folklore and urban legend.

Stories told to us by our friends who knew someone that knew someone that had something strange or frightening happen to them.

Stories almost always told after dark.

These are the stories that I wanted to collect and present to you in this book.

My purpose is not to pass judgment.

My purpose is to collect and present and hopefully inspire the kind of feelings that I used to feel when hearing a particularly well-told story of a supernatural experience by a friend of a friend.

It's always a friend of a friend.

So, please, wait until dark.

And now that it's dark, please go someplace comfortable.

And now that it's dark, and you're comfortable, turn off some of the lights.

Because sometimes it's easier to see when the lights are low.

And if the air around you grows cool, and you can feel a chill breath on the back of your neck, it's only the other side trying to say hello.

They've been waiting for quite a long time.

It's lonely being dead.

Guide for Urban Exploration

If you're anything like me, creepy looking abandoned buildings have an almost irresistible attraction as destinations for adventurous excursions.

Attractive destinations include abandoned buildings, usually the older the better, and especially asylums and churches, ex-military bases, and anything else interesting and off limits.

We all know that trespassing is illegal, but if you're as irresistibly attracted to these destinations as I am, there are a few things that you may want to keep in mind.

Many urban explorers bring back small souvenirs from their excursions. I still have two coffee mugs from the Ladd Center, which are precious to me. But I ask that if you do decide to visit someplace with the purpose of exploring it, that you avoid the urge to destroy or vandalize anything while you're there. Everyone loves the sound of breaking glass, and it's sometimes gratifying to leave your mark for future explorers to discover, but please think about preserving the site for other explorers. Vandalism only serves to increase security surveillance or make the site more likely to face destruction as a safety hazard and a popular destination for unwanted visitors. It's perfectly acceptable to take as many pictures as you desire, but the best souvenir will be your memory of the experience.

Things That You Might Want to Remember to Bring Along With You

Light

If your planned destination is a building, day or night, you'll want to bring a **flashlight**. If you enter an abandoned building, there will most likely be rooms that do not have direct access to the outside and will be dark without artificial light. It's also important to always be able to see where you're planning on going. The most common injuries for urban explorers are tripping over something underfoot because they weren't watching where they were going, or hitting their head or getting cut by something hanging down from overhead.

My favorite flashlight is the Mag-Lite mini. It's more expensive than the one-use flashlights that you can buy at the register or get for free as a promotional item with a pack of batteries, but it's infinitely more reliable and durable. It will survive a few accidental drops onto concrete floors, and the bulbs are cheap and replaceable. The light it throws is bright and clear and adjustable, and it's relatively cheap, so it won't be a big deal if you drop it someplace that you can't easily retrieve it. It runs on double A's and gets pretty good battery life, but **make sure you bring spare batteries**. You don't want to be trapped in an unfamiliar, potentially dangerous environment with a handful of dead flashlight.

Photography

A **camera** with a good flash is also highly recommended. Digital cameras are lighter and often cheaper than film cameras and can take a lot of pictures without requiring the user to play around with loading in a new roll of film in a dusty, musty environment. Plus, if you have to run, you don't want a bulky film camera with a flash attachment bumping around. Some of the most common sad stories about urban exploration are about broken or lost film cameras. Don't be one of those people.

Hair

Tying back long hair and wearing a baseball hat is recommended. You don't want your hair to accidentally get snagged on something and get pulled out. If you're going to hit your head on something it's better to get your hat knocked off than to get a rusty cut. Additionally, a stray hair flashed in front of a camera lens is frequently mistaken for evidence of the presence of the supernatural. A common and embarrassing error, and easily avoidable with a little precaution.

Attire

Wear **sensible shoes**. Sneakers with thick, skid-proof soles, or even better, work boots. The floors of abandoned buildings are often cluttered with debris and filth and sometimes damp or flooded. Also keep in mind that you may have to avoid wild animals or other hazards, so please be smart and tie your shoes. But only run if you're outside. Even a familiar spot might have changed since the last time you were there. Running in an unfamiliar environment is easily the best way to accidentally and possibly seriously hurt yourself while urban exploring.

You may want to bring light **work gloves**. Not so much to avoid leaving fingerprints, but more because abandoned buildings can be dirty places. There are rusty ladders and stairwell handrails and the walls are usually moldy. Anywhere you put your hands you can pick up dirt and you don't want that kind of dirt in your eyes or mouth. It's better to get your glove snagged on something sharp instead of cutting your hand open.

Just for Your Health

And speaking of mold and dust, if you're predisposed to allergies, you may want to invest in a good **dust mask**. In some old buildings there's lead paint dust and asbestos. I'm not too worried about breathing in a little toxic dust, but some of you may not be so careless.

The Legalities

Finally, as I've stated earlier, we all know that **trespassing is illegal**. If you're uncomfortable with possible legal involvement, there are many excellent places of supernatural interest that are perfectly legal to visit and explore.

It's important to keep in mind that even going onto property that is not public can be considered trespassing. If you enter an abandoned building, that can be considered illegal entry and trespassing. And if you had to do anything to a window or door to get into a building, it becomes breaking and entering.

If your presence as an uninvited guest is discovered, which sometimes does happen, remain calm. Don't make an awkward situation worse. Treat whoever apprehends you with due respect and politeness. Calmly and politely explain that you wanted to visit the location, but your intention was to explore and take pictures, while showing them your camera, not to break things and put up graffiti, and that while you were exploring you were careful not to accidentally damage anything and you are quite sorry and do not plan on returning. You might get your camera taken away, but that beats having to spend a day at court dressed in your really nice clothes and maybe having to do twenty hours of community service or something lame like that.

On a final note, I implore you to not bring any **weapons** along with you while urban exploring. Having a small pocketknife or pocket multi-tool like a Swiss Army Knife or a Leatherman can be convenient and handy, especially if your hair or clothes get snagged and you have to cut yourself loose. But it's completely unnecessary to bring a big hunting knife, or even worse, a handgun, along for the trip. If you're looking for ghosts, a weapon won't do you any good against them. Having a weapon just makes it that much more likely that someone will accidentally get hurt, and being discovered while urban exploring just gets more complicated if you're running around with a samurai sword.

Please be smart, be safe, and send me a set of your awesome pictures.

Or even better, take me a long on your next trip.

Chapter One
The DeFeo Murders
and The Amityville Horror

Like many people, the first word that came to my mind when discussing Long Island and the paranormal was Amityville. Twenty miles from New York City, two and a half square miles in size, with a population of almost ten thousand, Amityville is known for its pleasant location on the coast of Long Island. Amityville would have probably been content to be known for these common, everyday facts, but a tragic incident changed the reputation of this quiet coastal community forever.

Ronald

The story began with a young man named Ronald DeFeo Jr. Ronald DeFeo was troubled. Twenty-three years old, Ronald was known to use illicit substances recreationally and did not see eye to eye with his father who was a strict disciplinarian with a violent temper. These qualities alone would not have made Ronald exceptional in his time. What made Ronald different was that on the morning of November 13, 1974, at 3:15 a.m., Ronald walked from bedroom to bedroom of the Long Island home at 112 Ocean Avenue, and murdered his entire family with a .35 caliber Marlin rifle. Two shots for each of his parents, and as many for each of his four younger brothers and sisters.

After the murders, Ronald picked up the shell casings and dumped the rifle into the nearby Great South Bay. Later, Ronald burst into Henry's Bar and announced that when he came home from work, he found his entire family murdered in their beds. His friends returned to the DeFeo home and found Ronald's murdered family, and the police were called in to investigate the scene of this massacre. The next day, Ronald was the prime suspect, based on the police finding the empty box for the rifle used in the murders in Ronald's bedroom. That night, Ronald confessed to the murders after detectives wore down his attempt to portray the murders as a mob hit based on his maternal grandfather's involvements with the Columbo crime family.

Almost a year later, on October 14, 1975, Ronald went to trial for the murder of his family. The defense's insanity plea was ignored, and Ronald was found unanimously guilty of six counts of second-degree murder, each conviction carrying a twenty-five-to-life sentence.

It was during Ronald's appeal of his sentence that the story took on an even more deeply disturbing tone. Ronald claimed to have been the victim of harassment of a supernatural nature, which motivated him to commit the heinous murders. Ronald said that he was hounded by shadowy figures and disembodied voices, and that the harassment worsened until finally he became possessed by these evil forces, and it was the evil forces which had possessed him that compelled him to murder his entire family.

Understandably, the court failed to believe Ronald's story and upheld the initial sentence. Who could believe that a man had become possessed by demonic forces that compelled him to murder his family in cold blood? The house at 112 Ocean Avenue was left empty by the death of all but one of its residents and the consecutive life sentences to be served by the last remaining member of this unfortunate family.

The Lutzes

Enter the Lutzes, who moved into the house on December 18th of 1975. George and Kathy Lutz and her three children were pleasantly surprised to find such a perfect house in a beautiful neighborhood so affordably priced; their offer of $80,000 for the $100,000 house was accepted. But their pleasure soon turned to horror, and they lived there a short twenty-eight days before abandoning the house forever in the middle of the night.

This twenty-eight day stay has become legendary in the realm of haunted houses and in American folklore, and has unfortunately branded Amityville, an otherwise pleasant, quiet suburban neighborhood, as the foster home of what may potentially be, at best, a place where the boundaries between the physical and the spiritual are thinner than most, allowing the manifestation of a vortex of evil, or at worst, a doorway to hell itself.

The events experienced by the Lutzes during those twenty-eight days and the way their lives had changed after suffering through their ordeal has been the subject of several books, movies, and television specials. Thirteen listings for "Amityville" come up combining film and television sources when an informal search is done through the Internet Movie Database [http://www.IMDB.com]. Although this is a profuse amount of media covering one event, the manner in which the story is retold does not maintain consistency in retelling.

The simplest and least exaggerated retelling of the Lutz's ordeal seems to be this. After moving in, the Lutzes contacted a catholic priest to bless their new home in accordance with their faith. The priest arrived at the house, but while performing the ceremony heard a malevolent voice tell him to "Get out!" as presented in the 1979 film adaptation, directed by Stuart Rosenberg.

Kathy supposedly had difficulty contacting the priest to return and help the family with their paranormal problems after that event. The house was permeated with an indefatigable odor, which no amount of air-freshening could banish, green slime was said to ooze down the walls, and there were unexplainable manifestations of swarms of flies.

George Lutz reportedly found himself waking up every night at 3:15 a.m., which was the time that the mass murder had occurred in the home. George claimed that he found it impossible to stay warm in the house, and that objects in the house seemed to take on a life of their own, changing locations unexpectedly and seeming to be possessed by a malevolent awareness.

Kathy Lutz reportedly discovered an unusually painted crawl-space in the basement, which was called "the red room," which the family's dog, Harry, would bark at for unknown reasons.

The Lutzes youngest daughter, Missy, began playing with an imaginary friend named "Jody." Seemingly innocent and typically child-like, George Lutz found this unsettling when a rocking chair in his daughter's room would rock by itself when his daughter's new friend was visiting her, and George reports seeing eyes glowing red with evil intent from outside of the child's window.

After twenty-eight days, the Lutzes abandoned their house in the middle of the night, leaving all of their possessions behind. The house was subsequently investigated many times, most famously by paranormal investigators Ed and Lorraine Warren. [A website with a brief article about and pictures from the Warren investigation: http://www. warrens.net/amityvill.htm, and a link to the Warrens' New England Society for Psychic Research website: http://www. warrens.net/]

Since the horrifying events of the mid-seventies, the house has been owned by a few different owners, all of whom deny the presence or manifestation of paranormal activity.

Today

The house, a scenic Dutch Colonial house on the coast of Long Island's Great South Bay, built in 1925, looks a little bit different these days than it did during the mid-seventies when it established its reputation as a decidedly unfortunate place. Formerly 112 Ocean Avenue, the house has been reapportioned as 108 Ocean Avenue in an attempt to avoid unwanted attention by fans of the paranormal who continue to be attracted to the house as a destination for paranormal pilgrimages. The house has also been remodeled, but the remodeling reportedly has not been successful in completely obscuring the house's identity, and it remains recognizable to this day.

The events that reportedly occurred in this Long Island community have become inextricably burned into our collective consciousnesses as Americans. This connection has been reinforced by the presence and promotion of the story in both print and film. Initially presented in the 1977 book, *The Amityville Horror,* by Jay Anson, the story has gone on to inspire many sequelized novelizations, television specials, and film adaptations.

The problem with the Amityville incident stems from the intermixing of the factual accounts with the fictional. The factual events and the fictional legacy have been mixed with liberal freedom by novelists and film-makers making it difficult to extricate fact from fiction. A common myth about the Amityville residence, for example, is that it was built on an Indian burial ground. This is an untruth. Although there were Indian burial grounds around Amityville, there were none in Amityville proper, but this fallacy continues to be part of the myth surrounding the Amityville Horror.

In the end, despite the enduring appeal of the Amityville events as an attractive touchstone and modern example of the paranormal for haunted house fans, the truth will only ever be known by the people that claim to have actually experienced the events at the time that the events occurred.

Chapter Two
The Abandoned Lunatic Asylums of Long Island

When a mental health facility is unfortunate enough to be abandoned, it almost always becomes known as a haunted place. This should not be surprising, considering the air of fear and mystery surrounding people with mental health problems, and the places that treat them. The exaggerated extreme behaviors of people with mental health problems depicted in film and television does nothing to diminish the myths and mystery often surrounding the fields of psychology and psychiatric treatment.

Another reason that abandoned mental health treatment facilities are often thought of as haunted by the lingering presences of their former patients, is that the mental health treatment methods of the past seem inhumane when viewed in contrast to the treatment methods used today. The treatment methods of the past are also thought to be even more inhumane than they may have been when the history of mental health treatment is depicted in film and television. The depiction of the mental health treatment in history as inhumane is so common that it is almost universal, and thinking of a positive historical presentation of the mental health treatment methods of yesterday is practically unheard of outside of an educational setting.

It's easy to understand this trend in our society. Extreme behavior and extreme treatment methods are more interesting. The person who hears voices that tell him to murder his family is much more interesting, but exponentially less common than the person that goes through their whole life with depression or anxiety. Electro-Convulsive Therapy and the containment of patients in psychiatric wards with security measures similar to prisons are much more fascinating than people who take their psychiatric medications as prescribed and regularly visit a mental health counselor while living in the community and quietly maintaining an otherwise commonplace job and life.

But people with mental health problems are presented as completely, violently, and dangerously insane in the majority of our media. Multiple personality murderers, raving maniacs living in the streets, and serial killers are common stereotypical characters. Although there *are* people with mental health problems as extreme as those portrayed in film and television, they are thankfully a very small minority, or our society would be unable to function because of the violent unpredictability of the behavior of the insane.

The truth of the matter is one out of four Americans over the age of eighteen will seek the aid of mental health assistance each year, many seeking help with short-lived or relatively minor problems caused by situational developments in their lives, such as the death of their spouse or other beloved members of their family, or being the victim of a natural disaster, or suffering from any of life's many unexpected vicissitudes.

With the passing of time, the social landscape that the hospitals exist in change. Government policy regarding the administration of mental health service agencies and the methods of treating people with mental health problems change as new methods are discovered through social and scientific research and implemented by mental health treatment facilities. As this change occurs, the facilities that provide mental health treatment must change to match the changing governmental regulations and the changing needs of the individuals receiving mental health services.

Abandonment

The reason for the abandonment of many mental health institutions across America is not the widespread mistreatment of the patients of these hospitals, but instead widespread reform gradually refined through the second half of the twentieth century that decentralized mental health treatment and deinstitutionalized many patients, favoring a model implementing community mental health treatment centers and outpatient treatment and counseling.

As in most communities, Long Island has several mental health treatment facilities. These mental health treatment facilities perform a valuable service to the communities they serve by helping people experiencing manageable acute and chronic mental health problems to function as members of the community, and keeping individuals with chronic and severe mental health problems out of the community.

When a mental health treatment facility is no longer appropriate for the uses required of it, the facility may be remodeled, or if the expense of remodeling is greater than the anticipated cost of building a modern facility, the facility may be abandoned. An additional problem with renovating mental health treatment facilities is that the services provided by these facilities have unique demands, which make the remodeling of these buildings for other purposes difficult. This is not always the case, as in the example of Danvers State Hospital in Danvers, Massachusetts—featured in the film *Session 9*, and long a destination for urban explorers in southeast New England—which has been successfully redeveloped and remodeled into condominiums.

These abandoned mental health treatment facilities, because of their history and the legends which continue to thrive after their closure, make these structures attractive destinations for ghost hunters, urban explorers, and thrill seekers. The combination of the urban legends which have grown around these abandoned monoliths, the thrill of trespassing in the dark, lighting your way with flashlights, the changes inflicted upon the buildings by vandals, and the damage which occurs to a building through exposure to the elements and changes of weather, would make the exploration of any abandoned building an exciting adventure.

Most of these buildings would have seemed much less intimidating when regularly maintained, lit by electrical lighting and populated by its caretakers. But environments that may have seemed commonplace when they were in use often take on a mysterious and sinister persona when being rediscovered by urban explorers.

I remember from my own adventures in urban exploration of abandoned mental health treatment facilities, that commonplace locations like gymnasiums, classrooms, auditoriums, and swimming pools take on a strange new meaning when explored at night by flashlight. Even a boring hallway or stairwell can be scary when you realize how the flashlight fails to penetrate too far into their darkened depths.

Long Island is no different in the appeal of its abandoned psychiatric hospitals, and here are three of its most popular attractions.

Kings Park Psychiatric Center

Kings Park Psychiatric Center is located on the north-central shore of Long Island off route 25A. Established in the 1880s, and originally named Kings Park Lunatic Asylum, the hospital was founded on several hundred acres of land with three wooden houses that served as the original hospital. It was taken over by New York State around 1900 when the name was changed to Kings Park State Hospital.

Treatment for patients included rest, relaxation, and manual labor. It was thought at the time that the removal of patients from the stressors of city life, to a more congenial rural setting and engaging in meaningful work would help patients with their mental health problems. This changed when the population of patients rose beyond the hospital's initial capacity. Treatment changed as the census rose, incorporating new treatments. Electro-Convulsive Therapy, abbreviated as E.C.T. and commonly known as "shock therapy," and prefrontal lobotomies became common.

With advancements in the field of psychopharmacology, and the success of new medications in addressing some of the symptoms of residents of centralized mental health treatment facilities, treatment gradually altered, allowing many patients to live outside the hospital, taking their medications as prescribed and seeking assistance at community mental health centers when their symptoms became unmanageable. Kings Park Psychiatric Center closed completely in 1996. In 2000, the northern parts were turned into a state park and there is continued discussion of what to do with the remaining property.

Kings Park Psychiatric Center has reportedly long been infamous as a center for ghost stories and paranormal activity, although the evidence of this activity has yet to present itself. According to the stories, the center is haunted by the lingering spirits of hundreds of mentally ill patients that died in misery from mistreatment and torture.

Reportedly, visitors to this site have complained of dizziness and a feeling of absolute terror. There have been reports of cold spots, feeling like one is being watched, and unexplained noises. None of which really seem to be indicative of a paranormal manifestation and more than the excitement usually experienced by urban explorers when on a dungeon crawl of an exciting location.

Building 93, an imposing structure, is a frequent attraction, reported to be the home of beautiful wall murals done by the building's former residents. There are stories of screaming voices and tearful sobbing said to be associated with Building 15, also known as "Wisteria House." There are also reports of the cemetery, located in the northern area of the center, where a white humanoid ghost chases people away, seemingly in an attempt to warn them—and this same being was reportedly spotted around the campus and even inside one of the buildings.

An unusual attraction of this site is the underground tunnels, which are particularly desirable to urban explorers. These tunnels are responsible for a legend told of the location where many of the more unjust torture of the patient populace occurred, and therefore a fecund ground for the manifestation of otherworldly apparitions. There are even rumors that there are secret rooms in the tunnels where patients were tortured. But due to the attractiveness of these tunnels, they have been thoroughly explored and documented by urban explorers, and the presence of secret torture chambers have yet to be factually supported.

Central Islip Psychiatric Center

The Central Islip Psychiatric Center started out as a "farm colony" for New York City in 1889. The patients were transferred from crowded city asylums on Wards, Hart, and Blackwell Island. In time, the asylum was taken over by New York State and its name was changed to "The Manhattan State Hospital."

The campus was 1,000 acres and was the largest asylum by land area. It had over a hundred buildings, most notably a set of four groups all connected via corridors that stretched a mile long. That was called the "string of pearls," referring to its length and the superior quality of the building's designs. Therapy consisted in working on the farms or one of the many shops. The center had two rain spurs to serve the main power plant and the "string of pearls" and even had its own steam engine.

Visitors would also arrive by train, and the hospital had its own train station. By the 1980s, the state sold much of the property, along with the buildings, to the New York Institute of Technology and an industrial land developer. The college reused a group of the former psychiatric center buildings for dorms and classrooms, and the "string of pearls" was torn down. The land was redeveloped for a shopping center and industrial park, while other buildings were torn down to make way for the expansion of local suburban neighborhoods.

In 1996, the remaining patients were either discharged to live in the community, receiving treatment from community mental health centers, or moved to Pilgrim State Psychiatric Hospital. A few buildings have escaped demolition and remain abandoned. These are the most popular destinations for aspiring urban explorers.

Among the unusual phenomena reportedly experienced by urban explorers are inexplicable noises coming from the main hospital where treatment was administered to the patients. In the engineering building the sound of people screaming and moaning are reportedly heard and the apparitions of men working at the abandoned power plant, and a woman folding laundry at a lonely laundry table in the laundry building—all of which disappear when they realize that they're being watched, vanishing into thin air.

Pilgrim State Psychiatric Center

In 1927, New York Governor Alfred Smith, with public support, pressed the legislature to appropriate money to obtain a minimum of 10,000 beds needed to relieve overcrowding of existing mental health institutions. A hospital of this size had to be located out in the country where land was cheap and had to be as nearly complete and self-sufficient as possible, generating its own electricity, pumping its own water, and growing some of its food. One thousand acres in Brentwood was chosen for this to be established as a "farm colony," a popular form of therapy at the time.

Pilgrim State Hospital began construction in 1929, and was named after Dr. Charles W. Pilgrim, Commissioner of Mental Health in the early 1900s. Pilgrim State officially opened with 100 patients transferred from Central Islip State Hospital on October 1, 1931. Nine months later, 2,018 patients were hospitalized at Pilgrim. The number of residents varied over time, rising to its peak in 1954, with 13,875 patients.

At the time it was opened, Pilgrim was the largest facility of its kind in the world; in fact, it was the largest hospital of any type in the world, and its size has never been exceeded by any other facility.

The hospital community was independent in that it had its own water works, electric light plant, heating plant, sewage system, fire department, police department, courts, church, post office, cemetery, laundry, store, amusement hall, athletic fields, greenhouses, and farm.

The Pilgrim Psychiatric Center is the last of the large hospitals still open in Suffolk County. Kings Park Psychiatric Center and Central Islip Psychiatric Center were consolidated and relocated to the Pilgrim campus in Autumn of 1996. The following Autumn, the facilities were merged into Pilgrim Psychiatric Center under one name.

A parcel of land was sold to a developer who tore down seventeen identical buildings. The farming section of the hospital was sold off, renovated, and became the Western Campus of the Suffolk County Community College in 1974, and the taller buildings are still in use. There are dozens of buildings that still lie dormant. It should be expected that these abandoned buildings are those which are most attractive to urban explorers. There wasn't a lot about Pilgrim State, but one could presume that visitors experience "cold spots, feeling like being watched, and unexplained noises."

Chapter Three
Lake Ronkonkoma and The Legend of The Lady of The Lake

It's no surprise that American Indians or Native Americans hold such a firm place in our folklore. The gradual spread of European colonists across North America and their encounters and exchanges with its original residents was the foundation of American society. This expansion was accompanied by communing with the Native Americans, and many places in America still retain names which echo the language of the people who lived in America for centuries before the first European colonists set up their first tenuous settlements. The culture and customs of the Native Americans seemed alien to the European colonists, differing in many ways including religion and burial practices. This contrast of cultures has been fertile ground for stories both genuine and otherwise.

The Native Americans were far from a uniform culture. Social customs differed between the tribes, including lifestyles, language, and funerary practices. Some tribes buried their dead in mounds, while other tribal cultures buried their dead under funeral cairns, which are a mound of stones used to designate the final resting place of the deceased. Much has been made of the culture clash between the Native Americans and the European settlers. In particular, many uniquely American works of fiction and film have centered on the violation of sacred Indian burial grounds. It has long been established in our folklore that any building built on or near an Indian burial ground is likely to inspire, at the very least, the displeasure of the spirits of the dead, and misfortune of the supernatural variety is likely to fall upon the residents or visitors to these places.

The Legends

Lake Ronkonkoma is perhaps unique, since it is not the site of an Indian burial ground, but instead a rich variety of legends have grown surrounding this pastoral location.

Lake Ronkonkoma is the largest lake on Long Island. The lake is situated entirely in the town of Islip. The land surrounding the lake is in the jurisdiction of three different townships: Islip, Brookhaven, and Smithtown. As a result of the lake's existence, Lake Ronkonkoma was once a resort town, until the area experienced a population explosion in the mid-1900s. Remnants of old resorts and hotels can still be seen around the lake's shores. It is still a popular destination for Long Island residents, offering a variety of recreational activities to the public, including fishing, baseball fields, picnic areas, and opportunities to canoe on or swim in the lake. It seems that the enduring folklore and urban legends have not been able to frighten Long Islanders away forever.

The most well-known legend about the lake has retained its popularity to this day, although the particulars of the legend have changed over the history of its retelling, a common occurrence in folklore and urban legends.

To the Depths With Love

One version of the legend tells of a Setauket Sachem Indian who was not permitted to wed his beloved, a member of a different tribe. According to legend, the young Indian brave, in a fit of lovesickness, paddled his canoe out to the middle of the lake and killed himself by plunging a knife into his heart.

Another version of the legend surrounds a young beautiful Indian Princess who was in love with a white man, but forbidden to marry her European-American lover. Consumed by despair, she canoed out to the middle of the lake and killed herself. The princess's body washed to shore in the canoe, and was discovered by her lover, who climbed into the canoe and was swept away, never to be seen again by any living soul.

Yet another variation on the theme of star-crossed love, lakes, canoes, and divine intervention claims that before the white man arrived, there was a tribe of Secatogue Indians living in, what is now, Sayville. In this tribe, there was a princess who was in love with an Indian prince from the Poospatuck tribe, on the other side of Brown's River. Of course, the young, noble savages were forbidden to pursue their affair. One day they stole away to Lake Ronkonkoma and took a canoe to a romantic spot after nightfall to make love. The Indian spirits did not approve of this. The gods felt that people on opposite sides of the river, and consequently from different tribes, should not mix, and the gods saw their miscegenation as a crime requiring divine intervention. Their canoe sunk, and their bodies fell forever and ever down into the bottomless lake.

An even further variation on this variation on a theme suggests that the two lovers were to meet in the center of the lake and elope one night, but when the Indian girl rowed out to the middle of the lake that night, no one was there to meet her. Heartbroken and careless, she let herself drift and died on the lake.

And true to the notorious changeability of urban legends, another variation on the variation of the legend is called "The Troubled Spirit of the Lake" and tells the story of an Indian maiden who was convinced to sacrifice herself to appease the god Manitou. The determined maiden tied weights around her ankles, rowed to the middle of the lake, and slipped over the side. The maiden's lover, determined to follow her wherever she went, dove into the lake after her, and their bodies supposedly turned up in the Connecticut River weeks later.

In the longest retelling of the legend of The Lady of The Lake, in the middle part of the seventeenth century, an Indian Princess fell deeply in love with a young man of her tribe. She eagerly awaited her upcoming wedding day as she worked on the clothing she would wear, all the while dreaming of their life together. Of course, fate would not allow these star-crossed lovers to be together. One week before they were wed, her groom was murdered by a white settler from the nearby town of Ronkonkoma. The princess was inconsolable. She felt she could not stand to live without her love, especially since the man who killed her lover would never pay for his crime. Her family tried to help her, but they did not know what to do. They tried to speak to her, begging her to calm down, but their pleading only made her tears come faster. They left her alone by the fire, frightened by the depth of her grief.

On the night before what should have been the happiest day of her life, the princess rose and dressed in the gown she had made for her wedding and walked silently to the shores of the lake. She looked into the lake and was so heart-broken that she thought she saw her groom dancing just below the water's surface. The ghostly spirit seemed to call out to the princess using her childhood name. When she heard the name whispered by that voice, she called back to him three times, and swore that they would be together forever, and that united in the spirit world, they would get the justice they deserved. The princess then determinedly rowed herself out to the center of the lake, tied rocks to her ankles, and threw herself into the lake.

The suicide of the princess shocked and saddened her family and their neighbors, but despite their efforts, they could not recover her body from the lake. Some say her body now rests beneath a Connecticut river since the lake was bottomless and had a connection through the Long Island Sound.

The legend also says the lake has a strange depression near the northeastern shore, and weird lights and sounds are experienced as evidence that the princess is still grieving her murdered bridegroom. Others say that while her tormented soul was dying, the Princess vowed to avenge the tragic death of her lover, and once every year she appears on the shore, ethereal and lovely, still dressed for her wedding day. It is said on that day, she chooses a man to accompany her to the never-ending bottom of the lake to replace her lost love. According to this legend, every year at least one man drowns in Lake Ronkonkoma, and they are never seen again.

In a last, modern twist on the tale, every year a pair of lovers die in an automobile accident in the area, victim of the jealousy of The Lady of The Lake.

The longest story, as told above, reveals two of the other interesting legends surrounding Lake Ronkonkoma.

One of these legends is that lake is supposed to be bottomless, and rises and lowers mysteriously, without any noticeable relationship to local rainfall totals. It is even rumored to have secret underwater passages that stem for miles, ending in neighboring bodies of water, such as the Long Island Sound or rivers in neighboring Connecticut.

These legends are just that—only legends. The truth is that it is not bottomless. The lake has been reported as being between sixty-five and seventy feet deep at its deepest points. The lake is an example of a "a kettle-hole lake," formed by an isolated piece of ice which broke away from a glacier after it melted, leaving a depression behind. Lake Ronkonkoma is the largest kettle-hole lake formed on Long Island by the last glacier, which left the region about 20,000 years ago.

Another legend of the lake is that there has been a drowning every year due to the curse placed upon it. The vengeful spirit of The Lady of The Lake drags men to the bottomless bottom of the lake and the drowning victims return to haunt the lake and its surrounding area. It is also rumored, instead, that every year The Lady of The Lake drowns a young couple, pulling their souls to the bottom of the lake. Or that every year the lake sacrifices someone to their arcane gods. The Lady of the Lake calls young men out to the middle of the lake and drowns them.

It seems that in almost every version, the lady is an Indian princess who drowned herself in the lake. Unfortunately, drownings do occasionally occur where there are recreational areas that offer swimming, but someone dying every year at a swimming spot would certainly be noticed by the local chamber of commerce, and lifeguards would surely be assigned. There is a seed of truth at the root of this legend—people *do* drown. Like Onix Ariel Umanzor, one of a group of boys who was playing in the lake, trying to race each other to a buoy. He fell behind and disappeared, and was later discovered drowned. Perhaps he was just the victim of innocent youthful carelessness. But perhaps, instead, The Lady of The Lake continues to exact her revenge on the residents of Ronkonkoma.

Some Rationale for Lovers

Regarding the possibility that the Indian princess and her star-crossed lover were from different tribes living on opposite sides of the lake, there is historical evidence which helps to explain and discredit these legends. Lake Ronkonkoma was considered a most sacred place by the Indian tribes of Long Island and was also the meeting point of the different tribes that inhabited Long Island. Four of the thirteen tribes living on Long Island shared its shoreline as a common fishing station and meeting place, controlling different parts of it. These Indian tribes were known as the Nissequogues, Setaukets, Secatogues, and Unkechaugs.

These four tribes shared the privilege of using the river as a gathering place, but the tribes of the area did not live in the area immediately surrounding the lake, instead preferring to live near the coast of what is now known as Long Island. This historical evidence makes it seem unlikely that The Lady of the Lake and her lover fled from their respective settlements to meet in the middle of the lake.

But as much as time may pass, and the names of places may change, people stay the same. Young lovers will elope because their families do not approve of their union, and who can truly say that in the days before the white man arrived and swept across the land, that a young Indian couple did not secretly slink away from their tribes under cover of darkness during the meeting of the tribes at their sacred lake? Neither you, nor I, my friend, and this is why the Legend of The Lady of the Lake will continue to live on long after you and I have gone gently into the night.

Chapter Four
The Haunted Lighthouses of Long Island

Long Island's coastline is three hundred and forty miles long. This coastline is dotted with lighthouses that have served their coastline faithfully since their construction. Long Island is perhaps unique in possessing not one, but two haunted lighthouses gracing its shores, and a third in a nearby body of water. Lighthouses solitarily guarding their weather-lashed shores bring to mind the loneliness of their keepers and legends often arise of the dedication of these keepers continuing after their death.

Fire Island Lighthouse

Fire Island National Seashore is a popular tourist destination. A promotional site claims that, "Fire Island is unlike anywhere else on earth. With beautiful beaches, unique communities, dynamic culture of Pines and Cherry Grove and miles of boardwalks and walkways to explore." Fire Island also offers camping, hiking, swimming, surfing, boating, fishing, and has hotels and restaurants for vacationing visitors. But those in search of unearthly adventures have a different reason for visiting this scenic island.

The history of Fire Island goes back to 1653, when Isaac Stratford of Babylon built a whaling station named Whalehouse Point. Stratford and his crew would haul boats across the narrow sand island to the ocean and build towers from which a man could watch for the spouting of whales. When a spout was seen, Stratford would yell "Whale Off!" and the boats would be launched into the rough surf in pursuit.

In 1825, the federal government funded the construction of a lighthouse at the western tip of the island. The first lighthouse built on Fire Island was completed in 1826. It was a seventy-four foot high, cream colored, octagonal pyramid made of Connecticut River blue split stone. Built at the end of a barrier island, between the waters of the Great South Bay and the Atlantic Ocean, the first lighthouse was adjacent to the inlet. As late as 1856, a sailor passing through the Inlet could yell to the lighthouse keeper as they passed within feet of the lighthouse. But due to the westward migration of sand along the beach, known as littoral drift, less than 100 years later, the inlet is now approximately six miles west of the ruins, and four miles of sand have accumulated between the lighthouse and the western tip of the island.

The Fire Island Light was an important landmark for transatlantic ships coming into New York Harbor at the turn of the last century. For many European immigrants, the Fire Island Light House was their first sight of land upon arrival in America. The first Fire Island Lighthouse was not effective due to its height. It was taken down and the stone was reused to build the terrace for the present lighthouse. Today a circular ring of bricks and stone are all that remain of the original lighthouse.

Legend tells us that the lighthouse keeper at the time of the deconstruction of the first Fire Island Lighthouse was a Mr. Nathaniel Smith, who lived at the lighthouse station with his family. Lieutenant J. T. Morgan, the contractor building the new lighthouse, ran out of material and decided to take apart the old lighthouse and use those stones to save the cost and trouble of purchasing and transporting new materials and to avoid delays in the construction of the new lighthouse. The contractor convinced the Smiths to live in a wooden shack until construction of the new lighthouse was completed. Unfortunately, living on the coast of Long Island without modern amenities and exposure to the elements brought illness to the family and one of their young daughters died. Supposedly, the Smiths had to wait three days before a doctor arrived, and were forced to watch their daughter slowly waste away. The doctor arrived too late and some say you can hear a man moaning for the loss of his daughter. Others say you can hear footsteps on the lighthouse stairs.

A conflicting report states that the stone from the old lighthouse was used to build the terrace that the new lighthouse sits upon.

Another legend claims that one of the lighthouse keepers hung himself in the tower of the lighthouse, suffering from the loneliness of his solitary duties.

In an even grimmer turn, human skulls and other skeletal parts are reported to wash up on the beach in front of the lighthouse.

Although these legendary tales were all supposed to have occurred in the first lighthouse, it is the second Fire Island Lighthouse that seems to have inherited the hauntings from the first Fire Island Lighthouse.

In 1857, Congress appropriated $40,000 for the construction of a new tower. One hundred and sixty-eight feet tall, this tower was made of red brick, and painted a light yellow color. It was lit for the first time on November 1, 1858. The tower was changed to the present day-mark of alternating black and white bands in August 1891.

The United States Coast Guard has been present on Fire Island since its inception in 1915. A Coast Guard Station was established on the Lighthouse tract, and when the United States Lighthouse Service was dissolved in 1939, the administration of lighthouses was placed under the jurisdiction of the United States Coast Guard "in the interest of economy and efficiency" (Presidential Reorganization Act).

In 1964, a bridge was built across the Fire Island Inlet, allowing easier access, which aided Fire Island's tourism industry.

Despite this increase in tourism, the light of Fire Island died when the second Fire Island Lighthouse was decommissioned as an aid to navigation on December 31, 1973. The costs of maintaining a lighthouse were deemed prohibitive and the Fire Island light was replaced by "a small flash tube optic" atop the Robert Moses State Park Water Tower. After the Fire Island Lighthouse was decommissioned, the Coast Guard gave the National Park Service a five-year permit to use the entire Lighthouse Tract (approximately eighty-two acres). In 1979, the tract was declared by law to be within the boundaries of the Fire Island National Seashore. With limited funds, the major function of the Park Service, during its early administration of the lighthouse tract, was to prevent further deterioration of the buildings through neglect and vandalism.

Between 1974 and 1980, private citizens grouped together in an effort to "save the Fire Island Lighthouse." In 1982, the Fire Island Lighthouse Preservation Society was formed. They successfully raised over 1.3 million dollars for the restoration and preservation of the Fire Island Lighthouse.

In 1984, the Fire Island Lighthouse was placed on the National Register of Historic Places, and on Memorial Day, May 28, 1986, the Fire Island Lighthouse was relit and reinstated as an official aid to navigation.

In December 1996, the Fire Island Lighthouse Preservation Society, through an agreement with the National Park Service, took over the maintenance and operation of the Fire Island Lighthouse and Keeper's Quarters. Today, the light is lit by two 1,000-watt bulbs, which rotate in a counterclockwise direction, giving the appearance of a flash every 7.5 seconds. The lighthouse is seven stories high, 168 feet tall, and the light is visible for approximately 21-24 miles. Fully automated operation and maintenance of the light itself remains under the jurisdiction of the United States Coast Guard. In January 2006, F. I. L. P. S. took over the ownership and maintenance of the beacon from the United States Coast Guard. The beacon will continue to remain on all charts as a private aid to navigation.

The second Fire Island Lighthouse is still open to the public year round as a museum and offers guided tours of the lighthouse tower. The gift shop maintained in the second lighthouse sells a book on haunted lighthouses. The book, *Ghostly Beacons* by Theresa Schmidt, features the Fire Island Lighthouses. Employees at the gift shop say the stories are just colorful legends created to compliment the impression that the solitary seeming lighthouses impart to visitors when experiencing their quiet vigilance along the storm-beaten shoreline. Employees maintain that there is absolutely nothing paranormal about the Fire Island Lighthouses, old or new.

Not all employees are immune to the eerie effect of the legends, however. One woman remembers being scared to climb up into the tower when the electricity was out and said that you could hear "creepy noises." She admits it could be just the old building settling or wind, but she was still uneasy. There is a ghost tour held in October, and even the ghost tour guides get nervous scaling the tower in the dark. It is definitely scary enough to climb the one hundred and eighty-two steps of the long and winding spiral staircase where you can see through the stairs and contemplate how high you've ascended.

Stories circulate about heavy doors opening and closing by themselves, and the topmost windows rising by themselves, when a long pole is required to open or close them. There are also reportedly "strange" or "unusual" laughter and banging sounds that seem to come from inside when no one is supposed to be present, an "eerie feeling," inexplicable cold spots, and the appearance of a "shadowy figure" in the caretaker's house.

The truth about the Fire Island Lighthouses may never be known, but visiting the wind-whipped shores on a dark and stormy night is sure to be sufficient inspiration to fire one's imagination to dream about the life of Long Island's lonely lighthouses.

Execution Rocks Lighthouse

Execution Rocks Lighthouse is located on an outcropping of rocks in Long Island Sound. Built in 1850, the lighthouse was constructed to warn mariners sailing around the rocky shores off Sands Point, located off the north shore of Long Island near Port Washington. The brown and white-banded lighthouse stands fifty-eight feet tall, casting a flashing white light, which reflects in the waters approaching New York Harbor.

The evocative name of this lighthouse station is inspired by any of the several legends that have evolved around the rocks it is founded upon.

British Nautical charts gave the dangerous outcropping the name "Executioner's Rocks." The name bestowed upon these rocks by the many ships that ended their nautical careers prematurely by sailing their last voyage into the rocks, their fate the fault of insufficient lighting and heavy ship traffic.

A popular legend relates that, during the Revolutionary War, British soldiers abducted American rebels from their early American settlements, taking them to the isolated reef to be tortured and then executed. The British chose this secluded spot to avoid inspiring further dissent among the colonists. The British chained condemned prisoners to metal spikes driven into the rocks and let the prisoners struggle for their life against the rising tide, either drowning when the tide overcame them or leaving them helpless to defend themselves against the devouring by sharks.

In a contemporary twist, it is rumored that the U. S. Lighthouse Service relieved any keeper from duty without question. Not only because of the ghostly history of the rocky base the lighthouse is built upon, but also because serving as the keeper of this lighthouse was so lonely that it felt like a "sentence of death."

Local fisherman have continued to say that the disembodied spirits of those who died on the rocky reef, either by torture by the British or maritime misadventure, can still be seen on cloud-darkened nights from the surrounding storm-tossed seas haunting the shores of this lonely lighthouse station.

Race Rock Lighthouse

Race Rock Lighthouse is on Race Rock Reef, a dangerous set of rocks off the coast of Fisher's Island on Long Island Sound, at the mouth of the "race," where the waters of the sound rush both ways, depending on the ebb and flow of the tidal waters. At this point, the water surges with great velocity and force, and in heavy weather, the waves run dangerously high and have been the cause of many disasterous shipwrecks.

Race Rock Lighthouse was built under great difficulties. Francis Hopkinson Smith, was the designer of the lighthouse and the engineer for the project. He later became famous as a writer of lighthouse stories. A Captain Scott was in charge of the construction of the lighthouse.

By 1837, eight vessels had been wrecked in eight years on Race Point Reef. Finally recognizing the danger of this killer of ships, in 1838, Congress appropriated $3,000 for erecting a lighthouse at Race Rock—but the money was never spent.

In 1852, the Lighthouse Board reported that, "Various efforts have been made, and numerous appropriations expended, in endeavoring to place an efficient and permanent mark on this point. Buoys cannot be kept on it, and spindles have hitherto only remained until the breaking up of the ice in the spring." In 1853, $7,000 was appropriated "for a beacon on Race Rock." The funds were spent on installing a "daybeacon" which was completed in 1856.

In 1854, Congress appropriated $8,000 for the construction of a lighthouse station, but only $1,600 of this was spent, mostly on surveys. In 1869, $90,000 was appropriated "for a lighthouse at or near Race Point, Fisher's Island, Long Island Sound." After additional preliminary surveys costing over $6,500, an additional appropriation of $10,000 was made towards preliminary research in 1870. Based on the findings of the preliminary research, the lighthouse board estimated that it would cost approximately $200,000 to build the lighthouse. In 1871, $150,000 was provided by Congress.

The ledge on which the lighthouse was built is underwater and three-fourths of a mile from Race Point Reef. It has one larger and several smaller spurs of rock jutting out into the sound. The depths of the water within sixty-nine feet of the lighthouse is quite shallow, averaging between three and thirteen feet.

Construction of the foundation began in April 1871. Ten thousand tons of granite were used in the foundation. In 1872, the lighthouse board reported that, "The proposals for the construction of the foundation and pier of this structure were so excessive in rates and so much above the amount of the appropriation on hand had been expended that no more than the landing and the enrockment of the foundation, and two courses of the pier, could be contracted for."

In 1873, Congress appropriated a further $75,000 towards the construction of the lighthouse. Once the foundations were secure, a landing pier, fifty-three feet long and twenty-five feet wide, was constructed of heavy masonry to grant access to the lighthouse.

The lighthouse, including the keeper's quarters and the tower, were built in only nine months. The lighthouse keeper's quarters are relatively small compared to the tower, a squat one and a half stories high, but from the center of its front the granite light tower ascends. The lighthouse's tower stands sixty-seven feet above sea level and its alternating white and red electrical light, is visible fourteen miles at sea.

The total cost of the lighthouse was $278,716.33, and it was first lit in 1879.

Race Rock Light was automated by the United States Coast Guard in 1979, and it is still active to this day.

Race Rock Light is believed to be haunted and was investigated by The Atlantic Paranormal Society [TAPS] on an episode of their popular television show, *Ghost Hunters*, featured on the SciFi Channel. *Ghost Hunters* not only brought in excellent ratings, but also gave a high profile and easily accessible showcase for contemporary paranormal investigations, inspiring the growth of many existing regional paranormal investigations groups, as well as the founding of many more.

The show is a unique combination of chillingly unusual ghost stories, and high tech investigative methods. Many people watch the show, not only for the paranormal investigations, but also for the drama which plays out between the members of the investigative team, often having the same appeal as a soap opera for the show's many dedicated viewers.

Fortunately, I've known Brian Harnois from *Ghost Hunters* since high school. I called Brian to ask him about his experience when SciFi's *Ghost Hunters* visited the lighthouse to explore its paranormal activities.

Brian reported that there were unusual E.M.F. (electromagnetic frequency) spikes inside the lighthouse and went on to say that he heard unexplained voices whispering and murmuring indiscernibly around the investigators, and shadowy forms that dissipated when a light source was shone towards them. Most notably, a remote camera picked up a chair moving suddenly across a room when there was no one in the room.

Brian shared with me a conversation he had with the last lighthouse keeper before the lighthouse was automated in

1979. The lighthouse keeper related a story from his residence, where he and his fellow lighthouse keeper were in the living room when the lighthouse's shower turned on without anyone present in the area. They didn't think anything of it at the time, but when they went to investigate the bathroom after the shower had stopped, there was a trail of wet footsteps leading upstairs.

Chapter Five
The Mill Hill Windmill
of Southampton College

Eastern Long Island boasts the largest surviving collection of windmills in the United States. Eleven in all, it still seems a small collection. Aside from remaining as charmingly picturesque decoration on the horizon, windmills served as valuable labor-saving devices, helping with grinding corn and grain, sawing wood, and pumping water.

Known historically as the Mill Hill Windmill, it originally stood at Southampton Village. It's been known as the Mill Hill Windmill, the Tucker Mill, and the College Mill, and was the symbol of Southampton College. The Southampton College Windmill sits atop a knoll overlooking Shinnecock Hills, and offers views of Shinnecock Bay, the Great Peconic Bay, and the Atlantic Ocean.

The three-story, gray-shingled windmill was built in 1712, and served the community faithfully for over a hundred years. In 1890, in response to advances in technology, the windmill fell into disuse. Captain Tommy Warren, the last of the mill operator intended to tear the windmill down and replace it with a barn.

Mrs. William S. Hoyt, the daughter of Abraham Lincoln's Secretary of the Navy, Salmon P. Chase, had fallen in love with the windmill and purchased it in 1890 to prevent the destruction of the charming historical landmark. A team of horses pulled the windmill to its current location on her property where Mrs. Hoyt used the windmill as a tearoom and playhouse.

Six years later, in 1896, wealthy textile manufacturer Arthur B. Claflin bought the Hoyt estate and the windmill became a guest cottage. An interesting footnote in the history of the windmill, during its incarnation as a guest house, was that it was home to playwright Tennessee Williams for a summer, who reportedly enjoyed his stay very much, and said that it was one of the most creatively inspired summers of his career as a playwright.

Claflin's daughter Beatrice loved to play in the windmill, but her affinity for the quaint playhouse was unjustly rewarded. Legend relates that while playing in the windmill, she fell down the steep stairs and broke her neck, dying instantly from her injuries.

While owned by the college, the windmill was used as a "social center," a residence for visiting faculty, and a small lecture room.

Students reported that the young girl's spirit haunts the windmill, her innocent face peering from its windows. Since she was a child when she died, only her head and shoulders are seen. The apparition follows passersby from window to window as they walk by, and sometimes an indistinct voice calls out to them. The windmill emanates a eerie "vibe," but the students felt that the spirit of the little girl was just lonely and looking for a playmate

The windmill still stands alone atop its hill, and visitors are encouraged to visit and keep a lonely little girl company.

Chapter Six
The Chilling Legend of Reid's Ice Cream Warehouse

Reid's Ice Cream Warehouse was located in Blue Point Long Island. It was a warehouse used to store ice cream from Reid's Ice Cream, a brand manufactured in Brooklyn, New York.

The warehouse was reportedly closed down in the 1920s, and remained standing in a gradually worsening state of neglect and disrepair until its deconstruction in 2003 to make room for the spread of urban sprawl as a new residential neighborhood was built on the ice cream warehouse's former location.

There are two urban legends that surrounded the abandoned ice cream warehouse. The more popular legend is about a nightclub, a man, and a woman.

A Deadly Meeting

In the early 1950s there was a nightclub called the Shoreham in nearby Bayport. It was a popular destination back in those days.

A local girl—the only name the legends give her is Linda—accepted a job as a dancer there. One night, she made the questionable decision to accept an invitation from one of the club's patrons, agreeing to meet him in the parking lot after she got off work. It's said that she said goodbye to one of the other dancers as she got into his car later that fateful night.

The man drove them to the ice cream factory, a secluded spot that was a perfect place to be alone together.

At this point, the path of the legend forks.

One account says she hesitated in allowing his eager advances, and when she objected, her lover persisted. A crime of lust, he raped and murdered her, leaving her lifeless body on the property of the ice cream warehouse.

Another account maintains that the couple was absorbed in amorous activity when a third person attacked them. The man was murdered outright, and the girl was violently raped and tortured to death with a straight razor when the rapist had slaked his desire. Her body was found on the factory's property the next day, while her lover's body was never seen again.

Some say they have heard a woman screaming and crying, and claim to have seen a ghostly woman walking across the abandoned property. One account even reports the ghost wandering across the street, startling innocent motorists. Sometimes the apparition seems quite real, while she wanders the scene of her violation and murder. In one extreme version of the account, the phantom walks towards her victims, tilting her head to the side so they can see the savage wounds inflicted upon her by the straight razor. Then, just when it feels like the nightmarish vision is close enough to reach out and touch the person, she vanishes into thin air.

A Young Boy's Plight

The other legend regarding the abandoned ice cream warehouse concerned a young boy who supposedly died there.

As with many urban legends, the finer details of the legend differ.

One version maintains that sometime in the 1970s, a little boy was playing in the abandoned ice cream warehouse. Playing on or around an old piece of machinery, he either fell to his death on the factory floor, or was injured by the ruined machinery and died from his injuries, scared and alone inside of an abandoned ice cream warehouse.

The other version maintains that the little boy was retarded, and that he would play on the railroad tracks and one of those times, for whatever reason, he failed to move out of the way of an oncoming train.

Either way, there are those who claim to have explored the warehouse before its destruction, and while exploring, they report hearing laughter, humming, singing, and the pitter-patter of small feet echoing through the main room.

Renewed Hope for Abandoned Building

It was believed that an unexplained fire was supposedly responsible for destroying the original building. Repairs were planned, but more mysterious fires followed each time an attempt to rebuild was set in motion. The owners of the property eventually gave up their plans to rebuild. They boarded up the factory and abandoned it to the vicissitudes of time.

Contrary to popular belief, the factory may have been boarded up, but it was not abandoned. In a local newspaper report, dating from 1992, the factory was reported to be owned and cared for. There was even mention of plans for renewed construction permits, which seem to have been stalled for several years.

In December of 2002, *For Sale* signs went up on the old factory, and by January, demolition was finally set into motion.

While Reid's was still intact, local investigators went to visit the site, and there were some contractors looking at the site. The contractors would not tell the visitors what their purpose for being there was, but once the visitors began relating the legends attributed to the site, one of the contractors said that explained what had happened to them earlier.

Earlier in the morning, while they were setting up, the large, heavy, loading dock door began to shake. It continued to shake and became more violent and impossible to ignore. One of the contractors went outside to check and there were no trains passing, nor was there any wind. After a while and without explanation, it stopped shaking.

One, perhaps, would think that, with the destruction of the long-abandoned ice cream warehouse, its phantoms would disperse into the ether, but a chilling account related by a man who was unaware of the legend brings into question the longevity of the ghostly residents of this place.

The man reports that while riding his bike around his neighborhood, he accidentally found himself among an area where new homes were being constructed. While in this area, he encountered the ghost of a woman. As chilling as an encounter with the otherworldly may usually seem, the appearance of this apparition was particularly frightening, because where her eyes should have been, instead, there were wide black holes which seemed to recede into eternity.

Chapter Seven
The Poltergeist of Herrmann House

In the Seaford, Long Island, house of Air France employee James Herrmann and his family, inanimate objects seemed to take on a life of their own.

The events began Feb. 3, 1958, at approximately 3:30 p.m.

Bottles of liquid starch, bleach, nail polish, perfume, shampoo, hair tonic, prescription medication bottles, and even holy water spontaneously unscrewed their caps and toppled over.

The manifestations initially came in short spurts, usually just one or two manifestations a day. But later that month, the manifestations grew in frequency and violence.

James Herrmann watched a bottle of medicine hop at least six inches across a bathroom vanity into the sink. Herrmann's wife, Lucille, actually saw one bottle spin off its top, turn on the shelf, and fall to the floor. The Herrmanns gave their poltergeist the nickname "Popper."

The Herrmanns weren't the only ones to witness the poltergeist. In fact, the Herrmann House Poltergeist continues to this day as the most thoroughly investigated and documented poltergeist haunting in history.

A detective assigned by the Nassau County Police Department to investigate the unusual events also witnessed the phenomena. Twice, when hearing noises in nearby and unoccupied rooms, the detective rushed to see if he could discover the cause for the noises. Once, he discovered that a sugar bowl in the dinette had flipped three feet, and another time, in the son's bedroom, a chest of drawers had tipped over and the boy's record player was spinning around the room.

During the same investigation, a reporter from *Newsday* reported that he heard a crash from the unoccupied living room, and they discovered that a porcelain figurine of a colonial man had been thrown ten feet across the living room, smashing into pieces against a wooden desk. The figurine was hurled with such force that it had dented the wooden desk. Fifty minutes later, hoping to see one of the events, he positioned himself on the living room couch facing Jimmy's darkened bedroom. Suddenly, a ten-inch cardboard globe, silently spinning, hurtled out of Jimmy's room and down a hallway, narrowly missing the detective investigating the house for possible explanations and bounced into the opposite corner of the living room.

A bottle of ink flew from the dining room table and smashed against the front door, spattering everything in the vicinity of its impact. A sugar bowl suddenly lifted off the kitchen table and crashed to the floor. And a British photographer saw one of his flashbulbs levitate from an end table.

A neighbor suggested that vibrations from an underground stream might be causing the movements, and the Air Force thought that vibrations from overhead jets were to blame, but a vibration detector set up by the Long Island Lighting Company found nothing out of the ordinary. Technicians from RCA, covering most of the radio spectrum, were unable to detect any abnormal signals. The head of the Hempstead Town Building Department detected no defects in the five-year-old house, in which only the Herrmanns had lived.

After the Nassau County Police Department admitted to being unable to find any logical explanations, Duke University had its premier parapsychologists investigate the extraordinary events.

The Duke parapsychologists originally thought that the manifestations were caused by psychokinetic energy generated by the teenagers, in particular the Herrmann's thirteen-year-old son, Jimmy. Their reason was that children are often at the center of poltergeist activity, especially adolescent children going through the changes that accompany puberty. But since many of the odd events occurred when the children were not at home, the theory that the children were the cause of the paranormal activity was ruled out.

Sixty-seven uncanny incidents occurred inside the troubled house before the unusual events suddenly ceased on March 2, 1958.

The Duke University Parapsychology team produced a forty-five page study delineating in detail the inexplicable phenomenon, excerpts of which have been published in almost every book on poltergeist activity. The report is on file at the university.

Chapter Eight
The Massapequa Hell House

Known as both the Massapequa Hell House and the Massapequa Satan House, this haunted house has developed a notorious and enduring reputation across Long Island.

This haunted house is unlike most haunted houses. Most haunted houses are in remote locations and visibly reflect the passage of time they've endured through their dilapidated condition. Often the deterioration of these rural attractions for supernatural thrill-seekers are worsened by their uninvited visitors, many of whom fall prey to the urge to leave a sign of their visit for future visitors. The Massapequa house is different. This haunted house stands right in the middle of a residential neighborhood.

Located off the Southern State Parkway, the house is described as unusually old when compared to its neighbors—a "castle-like house with drapes the color of blood in every window and a vintage model hearse parked in the driveway." The house's funereal appearance is heightened by a "red-painted sidewalk in front" and a towering metal fence that surrounds the entire house.

Aside from the general appearance of the house, which seems more than enough to have earned it an unusual reputation, a variety of urban legends have flourished to enhance its notoriety.

Urban Legend?

Part of the legend is rumored to have been based on informal reports from volunteer firefighters who had occasion to visit the house.

One firefighter was supposedly a member of a response team called to the house to extinguish a fire set in the back yard. The firemen entered the house and were surprised and confused by what they observed. The interior of the house gave the crew the impression that the residents were practicing witchcraft, or at the very least, were interested in the occult. And inexplicably, a fence ran through the inside of the house.

On another occasion, they had to take the old woman living in the house to the hospital. She reportedly kicked and screamed and fought against the emergency response team, yelling and cursing at the ambulance driver, complaining that he was driving too quickly and recklessly. Inside the house, the windows were covered with funeral draping, which bore a striking resemblance to the material used to line coffins. There were disturbing graphic occult and satanic pictures in ornate frames lining the walls, and red candles lighting the house, as well as dark red shades on the lighting fixtures. The red lighting of the interior explains why the windows of the house seemed to glow red at night.

Even if the preceding stories are the products of overactive imaginations, the house continues to challenge the courage of high school students, especially around Halloween. Legend suggests that if you park your car outside of the house, and if the number of candles lit in the windows correspond to the number of people in your car, it is an ill omen, foretelling that one of the passengers in the car will die before a year has passed.

Why one would tempt the fates in such a way may seem ill-advised if one truly believed the legends attributed to this unusual house, but challenging the power of an urban legend in person has been and will most likely continue to be an integral part of the rite of passage or initiation of the American teenager.

Chapter Nine
The Haunted Mansions and Manors of Long Island

Long Island is famous for its many mansions that decorate what has come to be known as Long Island's Gold Coast. Many of these stately manors continue to house the spiritual manifestations of their owners, whose lives were often as interesting and impressive as the mansions they left behind as a living legacy of their opulent existence.

Morgan Hall and the Legacy of J. P. Morgan

J. P. Morgan & Co. was one of the most powerful banking houses in the world. It became the world's first billion-dollar corporation, and among the firm's numerous achievements was the formation of the United States Steel Corporation.

In 1909, J. P. Morgan, Jr. purchased the approximately one hundred and ten acre East Island property, in Glen Cove, located in northern Nassau County, with the intention of having a summer estate built which would allow him to enjoy the relaxing environs of Long Island's Gold Coast in relative privacy.

Morgan Hall was constructed in 1910. Contrasting with the island's pastoral environs, the interior of the estate was opulently furnished and decorated. The estate was representative of J. P. Morgan's reputation as a collector of books, paintings, and art objects. Morgan sponsored The American

Museum of Natural History, and The Metropolitan Museum of Art, of which he was president. Morgan also generously helped underwrite Harvard University, particularly its medical school, and several New York area trade schools.

In 1915, an unexpected event occurred at the estate when a German instructor named Frank Holt attempted to murder Morgan. The homicidal visitor fired two shots at Morgan, but was unsuccessful in his intentions due to the intervention of Morgan's butler. The murderer's motives were never clearly established, since he killed himself while imprisoned and awaiting trial.

Understandably concerned about the safety of his estate, Morgan had a "medieval style bridge and guard station" built to protect the entrance to his estate, and hired guards to occupy the guard station.

Fate was not content to leave the Morgans to enjoy their lives in peace. The Morgan's daughter, Alice, died of typhoid fever while residing in the estate—although the exact date of her demise and her age at the time of her death are unusually difficult facts to establish.

J. P. Morgan passed away in 1943, and the estate quietly became the property of the Russian government and was used by the Russian government as their embassy.

During the 1960s, the Russian Embassy moved to another location and the Catholic Church purchased the estate, converting the mansion into a residential school for girls and a convent.

The Beginnings...

The paranormal activity began to make itself apparent after the Catholic school girls and the nuns in charge of their matriculation and safety took residence. The nuns began complaining of loud disembodied footsteps echoing through the hallways and the attic throughout the nights. Windows on the third floor began to inexplicably and slowly slide open and just as inexplicably slam shut.

Originally, the residents of the nunnery and school presumed that John Pierpoint Morgan's spirit took up permanent residence inside his Nassau County Estate, and perhaps he resented having to share the home in which he spent the last days of his life. Indeed, the ghostly manifestation of old man Morgan floated through the students' rooms leaving an icy chill in its wake, terrifying the devoutly Christian residents.

The residents' opinion changed when the ghost of a young girl dressed in a long black gown was also witnessed. The spirit eventually managed to reveal herself to one of these novices, identifying herself as Alice Morgan, the daughter of J. P. Morgan who had succumbed to typhoid fever as a young girl.

One wonders why the Catholic church didn't take a more proactive approach towards the paranormal occurrences, considering that representatives of this religion are sometimes called in to dispel the lingering manifestations of the souls of the departed. Perhaps the nuns and their students felt sympathy for the soul of the young girl who left the mortal plane so early in life.

In time, the school was closed, the estate was abandoned, and was reportedly demolished between the years of 1980 through 1985.

The bridge and guard station Morgan had installed after the attempt on his life to protect the entrance to his estate are all that remain.

Winfield Hall: Was Frank Winfield Woolworth a Warlock?

Frank Winfield Woolworth began his career in retail as a clerk earning only $3.50 a week. Woolworth industriousness and tenacity paid dividends over time, and he opened his first store in 1879.

The Woolworth stores became an American institution. The stores sold discounted merchandise at an established price of five or ten cents which undercut other independent local merchants, who were still using the then common practice of haggling for the prices of their wares. Woolworth's stores also offered products for customers to inspect before buying, unlike earlier stores where merchandise was kept behind the counter and customers presented the clerk a list of what they wanted, which would be prepared by the store clerk.

Woolworth's five and ten stores also offered lunch counters that served as everyday gathering places, like an informal town hall, and the ancestor of the food court found in almost every mall across America. The success of Woolworth's methods did not go unnoticed by competitors and quickly became common practice.

In 1913, Woolworth commemorated his success by having the sixty-story Woolworth building constructed. The building's construction cost $13.5 million, which it is said that Woolworth paid in cash.

Winfield

At the time of its construction, it was the tallest building in the world, and remains one of the oldest and most famous skyscrapers in New York City's instantly recognizable Manhattan skyline. After more than ninety years, the Woolworth Building is still one of the fifty tallest structures in the United States.

In 1916, Woolworth's first estate on Long Island's Gold Coast was destroyed by a fire, but a man of Woolworth's determination, is not easily discouraged.

In 1917, Woolworth spent nine million dollars on the construction of "Winfield," (the number of rooms in the mansion vary depending on whose account one reads) varying from fifty-six to sixty-two rooms. The mansion was the definition of opulent excess, featuring a two-million dollar solid marble staircase, solid gold bathroom fixtures, a seven-foot-wide crystal and gold chandelier hanging down from a

1,500 square foot, fourteen–carat gold gilded, dining room ceiling. Other, more unusual architectural features such as secret tunnels, hidden chambers, and a concealed pipe organ reveal the somewhat eccentric character of it's owner.

Prosperity does not ensure longevity. Two years after the construction of his opulent estate, Frank Winfield Woolworth fell prey to an infection. The infection began with his deteriorating teeth, but due to Woolworth's phobia of dental procedures, he avoided seeking treatment and the infection worsened, becoming septic. In essence, Woolworth was gradually poisoned by the accumulating byproducts of the infection and his body's weakened immune system's inability to combat the worsening infection.

It had been rumored that during his brief residence in the mansion, Woolworth had an unhealthy interest in the occult and "dabbled in the Black Arts." It is reported that he kept a black mirror that was used in occult rituals, in his master bedroom—which begs the question of whether or not Frank Winfield Woolworth was a warlock.

In a further blight upon the history of the estate, one of Woolworth's three daughters, Edna, took her own life while residing in there. Legend claims that the family's coat of arms, featuring the faces of the family in bas-relief, was struck by lightning, and cracked through the face of Edna the night she killed herself. This seems more than a coincidence.

A Legacy Continues

In 1929, the estate was purchased by the Reynolds family. The notorious Reynolds Aluminum Foil was invented in a laboratory in the Winfield garage.

After the death of Mr. Reynolds, Mrs. Reynolds continued to reside on the estate until the costs of maintaining the elaborate home motivated her to sell it. The mansion then housed the Grace Downs School for Girls, a modeling academy and finishing school, from 1964 to 1977. The estate eventually went up for public auction.

While attending the public auction, Oyster Bay resident Monica Randall met Mr. Andre Van Brunner, a mysterious businessman who bought the ill-fortuned estate. After a whirlwind romance, Randall became engaged to Winfield's new owner, and moved into the opulent estate.

Monica Randall, an avid paranormal enthusiast, authored *The Mansions of Long Island's Gold Coast*, and also wrote *Winfield* (2003), which in addition to chronicling Woolworth's eccentricities, also serves as an account of her nightmarish experiences while living in the mansion and recorded the history of paranormal happenings at the palatial estate.

Almost anyone who worked or lived at Winfield, and some of the charm school students, observed the manifestation of a female spirit wearing a faded blue dress strolling through the garden and in some of the upstairs bedrooms.

It is also said that "the Italian Renaissance style mansion provided the perfect backdrop for the supernatural strains of spectral organ music that can be heard echoing through the spacious structure" on certain ominous evenings.

A psychic investigating the estate claimed it was full of negative spirits, and subtle energies that drained and tormented its living residents. The misty apparitions of Woolworth and his suicidal daughter appeared during a séance held in the mansion.

The psychic further informed the mansions owners that Randall, who resembled a woman who had scorned Woolworth in life, inflamed the wrath of Woolworth's wraith by taking the woman's room as her own.

The mansion is built almost entirely of marble, which contains quartz crystals, silica, and ferric salts. These materials are used in making recording equipment. Scientists and paranormal investigators speculate that marble and other similar materials containing crystalline deposits can trap a variety of energies for an indefinite period. These energies, under the right conditions may be released, manifesting themselves similarly to the manner that visual and audio information is captured on and played back from film stock.

Woolworth's spiritual energies are thought to have been so intense that they stayed behind, captured in his mansion because he refused to accept his death as the finite end of his existence. The same force of character that enabled him to persevere and succeed against adversity in life seems to have become infused into his earthly home.

Montauk Manor: The Many Lives of the Miami Beach of the North

Signal Hill had long been a prominent landmark in Long Island's South Fork.

During the days of Indian inhabitation, the site was an ancient Indian stronghold. Below Signal Hill lies "Massacre Valley," where the Montaukett tribe waged war with the Narragansetts in 1654. The Montaukett Indians buried their fallen warriors on what they called "Great Hill," and their descendents claim that when developers created Montauk Manor they desecrated "the most significant Native American burial ground on the Northeast coast." Perhaps this helps to explain some of the paranormal phenomenon observed at this impressive estate.

Later in Long Island history, in the 1890s, Theodore Roosevelt reportedly escorted a regiment of soldiers suffering from yellow fever to the site for rest and rehabilitation. Many soldiers from this regiment were unable to overcome the disease and, after their death, they were temporarily interred atop the tribal remains.

But despite the rich history of Signal Hill, it is Carl Fisher who may have made the most enduring impression on Montauk. Carl Fisher was an industrialist and land developer who earned his fame by developing Miami Beach out of a mangrove swamp.

Fisher also left his mark on the plains of Indiana, by establishing the Indianapolis Speedway. Located in Speedway, Indiana, with seating for 255,000, the Indianapolis Speedway is the largest, highest capacity, sporting arena ever to exist in the history of mankind.

In 1926, the multi-millionaire and four partners focused their collective interest on Signal Hill. They collectively purchased 9,000 acres on the Montauk peninsula with the intention of building "the most fabulous summer resort ever imagined in the world."

Plans for the "Miami Beach of the North" began with creating Montauk Harbor. Fisher had a channel dredged between Great Pond and Block Island Sound to create a marina to launch the resort's yacht club.

The resort features as its centerpiece an English Tudor-style estate, which has been described as a "one hundred and seventy-eight room lodge" and a "200-room luxury resort hotel" which was, during the height of its success, a popular destination for the rich and famous.

The exclusive, yet popular, resort featured a beach club, a yacht club, a half-mile boardwalk along the ocean, polo fields, a golf course, glass-enclosed tennis courts, a health spa, and even a ranch. Restaurants featured impeccable service and internationally acclaimed cuisine.

All of this changed in 1929 when the Great Depression forced his development company into bankruptcy. The resort experienced a revival in 1933 and operated for thirty years as a hotel, but over time, financial difficulties forced Montauk Manor to close its doors.

For over twenty years the brooding behemoth sat empty atop its elevated outlook, a victim of vandalism and the vicissitudes of weather.

In 1981, investors rescued the deteriorating property and by 1985 a twenty million dollar restoration project was completed. Montauk Manor regained its original splendor and beauty.

Odd Happenings

Perhaps sometimes it is better to leave the places of the past to exist in our memories. The restoration of Montauk Manor seems to have rekindled more than the memories of the manor's previous splendor. Soon after the manor's restoration, reports began to come forth of odd occurrences at the revivified vacation destination.

Unusual happenings have been reported occurring on all floors, mostly during the off-season when the resort is less crowded, and mostly at either dawn or dusk, or during the night, which is no surprise considering it is at these times that the boundary between the everyday world and the world of the supernatural are supposed to be at their thinnest.

According to one report, a female staff member saw a figure, described as a tall man, with long white hair, and "bathed in light," walk past a doorway into an *Employees Only* area. Thinking that someone other than an authorized employee was entering the locale, she ran to follow the man, but when she entered the area, he was nowhere to be found.

One guest, wrapped in a towel, ran to the lobby and reported a pair of evil eyes peering down at him from a heating vent as he showered.

A female resident claimed that one night her bed rose five feet off the floor. This would have probably been less terrifying is she hadn't been in the bed at the time. Who would blame her for requesting she be moved to a different room? Hotel staff, familiar with the hotel's unusual occurrences, complied with the woman's request without question.

The most famous of the phantoms witnessed at Montauk Manor would have to be the Indian chief. According to the popular tale, a guest awoke to find a Native American in full headdress standing at the foot of his bed. The guest screamed in fright and his two roommates, awoke by his screams, also witnessed the apparition, who suddenly disappeared from sight.

One particularly interesting Labor Day weekend, representatives from the Montauk Indian tribe asked permission to erect a teepee in the hotel's parking lot as part of a ceremony intended to put to rest the spirit of the Indian chief. The intention was to set the teepee alight, which would help to satiate the chief's lasting presence at the resort. The hotel, understandably, declined to grant permission, knowing that it would be in direct violation of local fire codes.

All things said and done, the ceremony may not have been necessary. The reports of unusual occurrences have become less frequent with the passage of time. Maybe the strength of the spirits haunting the hotel continues to wane. But then again maybe there will still be those sensitive to paranormal presences who will witness the restless soul of the chief of the Montauketts guarding the site of his tribe's most memorable defeat.

Meadow Croft and the Eternal Residents of The Roosevelt Mansion

Meadow Croft, also known as The Roosevelt Mansion, is located on Middle Road in Sayville, New York.

The estate occupies a large tract of land in the middle of the Suffolk County Sans Souci Lake Nature Preserve, which divides Sayville on the west from Bayport on the east, also dividing the east and west branches of Brown's Creek which flows into the Great South Bay.

The approach to the estate is reportedly "among the most haunting and beautiful on Long Island, over a narrow concrete bridge and up a long dirt drive embedded in tall marsh grass." Further, one source poetically relates that, "Waving in the wind, this grass beckons the visitor back to the Gold Coast period, for Meadow Croft exists in a remarkable state of preservation evocative of the first third of the twentieth century when it was last occupied."

Meadow Croft is an early Colonial Revival residence designed by Isaac Henry Green (1858-1937), one of Long Island's most important Beaux Arts. The Dutch Revival style, beginning in the Hamptons as early as the 1890s, is exemplified in Meadow Croft, especially by the Dutch double doors of the main foyer, which may refer to the Dutch ancestry of the Roosevelt family.

As the Long Island home of the Roosevelt family, a very important family in American history, Meadow Croft carries a unique historical importance. Three Roosevelts are most prominently associated with the estate.

Robert Bamwell Roosevelt (1829-1906) purchased the land on which Meadow Croft sits. He was an important New York State reform politician, a United State Congressman from 1871 to 1873, and one of America's earliest conservationists. Meadow Croft's present status as part of the Sans Souci Lake Country Nature preserve perpetuated the conservational interests of the Roosevelt family.

His nephew, President Theodore Roosevelt (1858-1919) often visited the property, and a cousin of the President, (John Ellis Roosevelt, 1853-1939), who was also a legal advisor to the President, commissioned the estate in 1891.

President Theodore Roosevelt is well-known nationally and internationally as the colorful leader of the "Rough Riders" in the Spanish-American War, Progressive Republican Governor of New York from 1899 to 1900, President of the United States from 1901 to 1908, and Nobel Peace Prize winner in 1906.

John Ellis Roosevelt was a well-known New York City investment banker and an active contributor to Long Island's social life through his participation in clubs and sports such as cycling and sailing.

The paranormal happenings at the estate are relatively minor in comparison to the historical impact of the Roosevelt family.

There is a feeling of unnatural coldness and overwhelming sadness reported emanating from the dining room and Mrs.

Roosevelt's bedroom, as experienced by individuals sensitive to the lingering presence of the spirits of the departed.

Local legend indicated that the mansion is set back in a swamp, and for quite some time was in disrepair and that the grounds were overgrown. There were strange rumors of a man that would roam the swamps, protecting the house. Some even suggested that it was the vigilant manifestation of President Roosevelt himself.

Chapter Ten
The Historical Haunted Homes of Long Island

Perhaps not as notoriously infamous as the Herrmann House or the Massapequa Hell House, or as resplendent or evocative of one's imagination as the mansions and manor houses of Long Island's "Gold Coast," there are many smaller historical homes and private residences that are haunted by their past residents and the events that therein occurred.

The Many Lingering Spirits of Raynham Hall

A website promoting Raynham Hall states that:

"Raynham Hall is a twenty-room house museum that transports you back into the life and times of the Townsends, one of the founding families of the Town of Oyster Bay on Long Island, New York. Unfolding history from the American Revolution in the 1770s through Oyster Bay's affluent Victorian period in the 1870s, Raynham Hall was accredited by the American Association of Museums in 1991. It is the only house museum on Long Island to earn this high honor. The Museum is open to the public year-round for visits, tours, educational programs and research."

Raynham Hall, a white saltbox house, sits on Oyster Bay's West Main Street as it has for almost three hundred years. Its history dates back to 1740 when it was center of local affairs in Oyster Bay and home to the affluent and influential Townsend family and members of George Washington's Culper Spy Ring.

This historical house played an important role in the Revolutionary War, both for and against the British.

This home quartered British troops during the British occupation of Oyster Bay in 1778, as was the law in the American colonies.

John Andre, a British major during the Revolutionary War, spent many hours at Raynham Hall visiting with the Townsends who were quartering the British Commander Colonel John Simcoe.

One day as Andre conferred with Simcoe, Sally Townsend overheard them scheming about a bribe that would be paid to General Benedict Arnold in exchange for the surrender of the troops and the military installation under his command.

General Benedict Arnold, in reward for his bravery at Saratoga, was placed in charge of West Point, a vital fortification on the Hudson River, positioned to protect northern New York from attack. Benedict Arnold, believing that he had not received enough recognition for his services, plotted with John Andre and John Simcoe to turn the fort over to the British.

Through their connections, the Townsends relayed news of the treasonous plot to then General George Washington. Fortunately for America, Benedict Arnold's scheme was thwarted when John Andre was caught red-handed with Arnold's letter. John Andre was executed and Benedict Arnold fled to England for refuge and died in London in 1801.

House Personalities

Perhaps it was the importance of the events which took place here, and their impact on American history which have infused the house with the personalities of those who frequented the house during their lives, compelling their spirits to linger long after their deaths.

The most famous ghost of Raynham Hall is supposed to be the spirit of Sally Townsend. According to romantic legend, she had fallen in love with John Simcoe, and history documents that he returned her affections. Regardless, Simcoe betrayed her affections when he left with the British forces who had been occupying Oyster bay, escaping the fate which ended the life of co-conspirator John Andre. Sally remained unmarried, a bitter spinster, dying unhappy at the age of eighty-two.

Sally's bedroom, on the second floor, is always icy cold, even during the summer. It gets so cold in the bedroom that museum staff wear warm coats whenever they venture inside. Paranormal investigators have said that this room makes you feel anxious. It's as if there's a weight on your chest. The room has a powerful oppressing feel.

The spirit of Sally Townsend isn't the only perpetual resident of this historical house. In 1913, Julia Weeks Cole purchased Raynham Hall, living there till 1933, and she was the first to document the hauntings. In 1938, Julia wrote that she awoke in the middle of the night, looked out the window and clearly saw a man on horseback. She suspected it was the spirit of Major John Andre returning to the site where his treachery was discovered.

There is also an annually-appearing apparition. A shaggy looking young man, wearing a dark woolen coat with brass buttons and smoking a pipe, walks in the garden.

One October, a volunteer working in the Raynham Hall yard saw the ghost, walking fully visible out of the house into the garden to which the door exits. When Andrew Batten, director of Raynham Hall Museum, who was also in the yard, looked up, he saw the door swing shut. Batten recalls thinking, *It's strange, since there was not supposed to be anyone inside, and all the museum's alarms were set.* In the following March, near the main staircase of the house, a weekend worker saw a thin man with facial hair, wearing a dark "drapey jacket," appear with the bottom half of his body missing, and another time as a full-body apparition. Staff theorize that this is the spiritual manifestation of Michael Conlin, an Irish immigrant who worked at the home as a servant in the 1860s.

As if three ghosts were not enough for the former home, on another occasion, a curator was working late one night in Raynham Hall's upstairs office and had an unusual encounter with the residents of the hall. Museum director Andrew Batten reports that, "Someone or something kept pushing a door into her. As we were the only ones here, she was sure I was playing a joke on her. After about five or six times, she burst out of the room, trying to catch me. She screamed when she saw that I had actually been on the first floor, and was only then coming up the stairs." Investigators suppose that this mischief is the manifestation of the ghost of a young boy, and that he is often to blame when doors in the museum open and close inexplicably.

The supernatural manifestations are not exclusively visual. Some visitors report the lingering odor of a whiskey, pipe tobacco, and a rose-scented perfume. There is also the scent of apple and cinnamon or fresh-baked apple pie in the kitchen, and if you smell it, legend claims that it is a sign that you have been welcomed by spirits of the house.

Others feel less than welcome when visiting the Raynham Hall Museum. Some claim that the feeling of being watched is overwhelming. The mannequins set by the museum's curators, dressed in period clothes and posed to illustrate scenes of daily life during the revolutionary era, probably do little to assuage the visitors sense of supernatural surveillance.

Nicholas Bain and the Axe Murders of Wickham Farmhouse

Located on the east end of Long Island on the Peconic Bay, the Cutchogue Green Historic Buildings complex includes the Wickham House. Built in 1740, it is one of North Fork's, as well as one of New York State's, oldest English style houses. Just over a hundred years into its history, the house was home to an unexpected multiple murder.

Nicholas Bain was an Irish farmhand. Bain worked on the Wickham farm but he could not handle his liquor and was known to harass the servant girls. Bain asked one of the girls to marry him, and when his proposal was rejected, his resentment remained strong and resulted in his being fired. After his firing, Bain continued to linger around the farm and harass the object of his desire. Nicholas Bain was forcibly removed from the farm by its owner, James Wickham.

Nicholas Bain did not forget his treatment and his anger would not allow him to forgive. On June 2, 1854, in a fit of insanity, he murdered James and Francis Wickham in the master bedroom of the house. Nicholas hacked them to pieces with an ax and also murdered a servant boy. The record of the account is particularly gruesome.

"Mr. Wickham lay weltering in his blood, his head literally cut to pieces. Mrs. Frances Wickham, his wife, was dead, she having had her brains completely knocked out, which, together with her blood was scattered about the room."

Bain had left his hat behind as irrefutable evidence of his perpetration of the crime. An extensive manhunt, comprised of men with pistols and rifles, was launched and Bain was found hiding in a nearby swamp, the bottoms of his pants soaked with the blood of his victims. Although the angry mob wanted to hang him upon the moment of his discovery, the sheriff intervened and Nicholas Bain went to trial. Bain was convicted of first-degree murder. On December 15,

1854, Nicholas Bain was hanged from the neck until dead as punishment for his crimes, his body buried in an unmarked grave.

The Bain Wrath

As tragic as the event was, it's human nature to try to forget tragic happenings in the past with the passage of time. But Nicholas Bain's wrath was so powerful that it left an indelible impression upon this formerly quiet farmhouse.

The farmhouse remained in the Wickham family, and, in 1988, family descendants awoke to view the ghostly manifestation of Nicholas Bain standing at the foot of their bed brandishing an axe. Although the phantom promptly disappeared, in response to the panicked reaction of the couple, they decided that one visit from beyond was enough, and they sealed off the room and moved into another bedroom.

The farmhouse continues as a private residence, but the master bedroom remains sealed. Members of the family have decided that as far as they're concerned, the unearthly apparition of the murderer can keep the bedroom for the rest of eternity.

Even though the master bedroom remains sealed, the sound of Nicholas Bain's footsteps as he walks down the second story hallway can still be heard.

It seems that some spirits will never resign themselves to quietly becoming a footnote in history, and the gruesome story of the Wickham murders is retold year after year during Halloween hayrides hosted near this haunted home.

The Woodward Estate and the Unfortunate Death of William Woodward.

On the night of October 30, 1955, tragedy struck the Woodward home.

William and Ann Woodward returned to their weekend estate in Oyster Bay on Long Island, after attending a dinner party in honor of the Duchess of Windsor. There had been reports of a burglar victimizing homes in their neighborhood. The couple retired to separate bedrooms, but both were armed with loaded weapons.

Awakened by the sound of their dog barking, and what she later described as the sound of an intruder, Mrs. Woodward grabbed the double-barreled shotgun by her bed and fired both barrels at a shadow in the hallway. The shadowy form was her husband. One of Ann's shots hit her husband in the neck, virtually decapitating him. Ann reports rushing to her husband in horror, and calling the police. Their two sons, ages eleven and seven, were asleep in another part of the house, and thankfully slept through the sound of the blast that prematurely ended their father's life.

The shooting instantly became front-page news. *Life* magazine dubbed it "The Shooting of the Century." Distraught and visibly anguished, Mrs. Woodward appeared before a Nassau County grand jury, but was exonerated when the grand jury determined that the shooting was a tragic accident. But the family would never be the same.

Members of New York Society's elite gossiped that Ann deliberately murdered her husband, and that her mother-law, Elsie Woodward, covered up the crime to prevent further scandal from staining the reputation of the socially prominent family. As a result of these ill-spirited rumors, Mrs. Woodward was ostracized socially and haunted by the whispered allegations of her former friends.

For decades the controversy continued to circulate over whether Ann intentionally murdered her husband. The allegations came to the attention of Truman Capote, whose unfinished, but published, novel, *Answered Prayers*, included a thinly veiled fictional account of the Woodward shooting. He thinly disguised Mrs. Woodward as Ann Cutler, a harlot and "gold digger" who killed her husband because she had discovered he was a bigamist, or a man that is married to more than one woman at the same time. In 1975, Esquire published an excerpt from the novel, and New York society quickly accepted Capote's fictional account as fact. Ann Woodward could no longer bear to live in infamy and she was discovered in her Fifth Avenue apartment, after a successful attempt at suicide.

"Well, that's that," said Elsie Woodward, then in her 90s, said six weeks after Ann's death. "She shot my son, and Truman just murdered *her*, and so now I suppose we don't have to worry about that anymore."

The family saga resurfaced when another fictional account of the shooting, *The Two Mrs. Grenvilles* was penned by Dominick Dunne. The book was published in 1985, and was later made into a television movie.

Family Tradition

As a sad example of the way that this family was irrevocably changed by the sudden death of William Woodward, both of the sons of the ill-fated family followed their mother by committing suicide.

The younger son, Jimmy, died first. Jimmy dabbled in drugs and spent time in mental institutions. He attempted to end his life by jumping out of a fourth floor window, but survived. Less than a year after his mother's suicide, Jimmy jumped out of a window of a hotel on Central Park South and succeeded where he had previously failed.

Years later, the older son, William Woodward Jr. jumped through the kitchen window of his East Side apartment, falling fourteen stories to his death.

The estate became famous because of the death of William Woodward and the pall his murder cast upon the family. Legends circulated that the spirit of William Woodward lingered in the estate, his nearly headless ghost protecting the home from uninvited intruders like the one that inadvertently cost him his life.

On the twenty-seventh anniversary of the shooting on Halloween Eve, 1982, Dominick Dunne, author of *The Two*

Mrs. Grenvilles, and Monica Randall, author of *The Mansions of Long Island's Gold Coast* and *Winfield* visited the Woodward estate with a psychic to perform a séance. Randall reported, "We were sitting around and joined hands in a séance situation, about twelve feet from the actual shooting, and a World War II medal materialized out of nothing." Randall confirmed that William Woodward had indeed won the same variety of World War II medal.

Chapter Eleven
Paranormally Plagued Public Places

Aside from Long Island's glorious mansions and private homes known for their paranormal activity, there are also many places that are or were public businesses or gathering places. Some of these places have been unfortunate enough to witness unfortunate events where people died from unusual circumstances or saw fit to vent their envy and wrath by murdering those that they thought were the root of their torment.

These places continue to carry the memory of these events and ethereal reminders may be experienced if the conditions are right.

Country House Restaurant: Stonybrook

The Country House Restaurant has a long-standing reputation as a haunted restaurant.

Located in Suffolk County, the structure was a farmhouse built in 1710. It was used as a stagecoach station in the late 1800s. The structure became a restaurant in 1960.

History records an unusual incident occurring during America's Revolutionary War. A woman, variously named as Annette Wilson, or Annette Williamson, was left in charge of her home while her family was away in New Jersey. The British occupied the residence, this much is known, but here the story varies. One account maintains that the woman was executed by hanging under suspicion of being a spy by the British. In another well-researched account, put forth by Keriann Flanagan Brosky in her book *Ghosts of Long Island: Stories of the Paranormal*, the woman was murdered by townspeople after the British had moved on. It was thought that anyone that did not fight against the British to the death were Loyalists, sympathetic *to* or allied *with* the British. The townspeople supposedly hung the woman from the ceiling of her home. All accounts maintain that the woman is buried in a grave in a small neglected cemetery on the property.

A Spirited Restaurant

The spirit of the woman is alleged to continue to reside in what was once her earthly home, making the restaurant a popular site for paranormal investigators.

The owner, employees, customers, and people who have worked on the grounds claim to have seen various manifestations of the spirit, as shadows, or even a full-figured apparition. Even passersby have reported seeing a pretty, blonde-haired, blue-eyed girl in a white dress looking out from the window of the room where her execution took place.

The spirit most commonly makes her presence known in the vicinity of the main staircase or walking around the kitchen. Phantom footfalls are heard and objects move inexplicably when least expected. According to several reports, a towel floated in mid-air past several witnesses as if carried by an invisible waiter or waitress, and a skeptical news reporter had a glass of wine off a passing waiter's tray thrown in his face.

A psychic, investigating the rumors of the restaurant's residents, claims to have contacted the spirit of a young woman who verified that she was the woman who was unjustly executed so many years ago.

Normandy Inn: Bohemia

This building, popularly known as the Normandy Inn has a legendary history as a speakeasy during the prohibition era.

It is rumored that a woman named Maria was savagely strangled to death in the back bedroom of this hotel during it's brief incarnation as a backroom bar.

The ghost of Maria seems unable or unwilling to leave the place of her murder.

It is said that late at night her spirit can be heard walking up and down the halls. Guests claim that the spirit knocks on the doors of their rooms in the middle of the night. When they open their doors, they are greeted by nothing but a cool breeze.

Maria has been known to linger in the building's kitchen. Cold spots, whispers, and unidentifiable noises have been reported, along with her furtive shadow moving about the cook space.

The imprints of bare feet appear inexplicably impressed into the carpets during the winter months. The most famous example of this phenomenon appeared when new carpeting was being installed. The foam padding was installed and left uncovered overnight. The padding revealed a trail of bare footprints when the doors were opened the next day.

In a grim turn to this story, unidentified human bones were discovered in the basement of the building. Perhaps these are the final remains of the woman so suddenly and savagely shuffled off this mortal coil.

The inn has been investigated many times by a miscellany of mediums and psychics. The building is now home to an interior design firm.

The Lives and Spirits of 105 Harbor: Cold Spring Harbor

Cold Spring Harbor and this building have had many lives during its existence.

It began as a port during Long Island's history as a departure and arrival part for New England whalers. The building served as an inn and tavern for the crew of whaling ships while they were in port. The inn and tavern also developed a side business as a brothel. The brothel, in an ironic twist, was supposedly staffed by the wives of whalers while the walers were out working on the many whaling ships that sailed from the port. The wives were supposedly seeking the comfort of a warm embrace or the satisfaction of sexual urges while their husbands were away, risking their lives on the Atlantic to benefit the shipping and whaling industries.

This coincidence would have dire repercussions one time when a whaler returned earlier then expected from one of his voyages. While drinking in the tavern, the whaler discovered that his wife was working in the brothel and was at that very moment servicing a customer in one of the inn's upstairs rooms. The whaler went upstairs and murdered his wife and her customer, recorded in the legend as a Mr. Van Whether.

The spirits of the murdered couple were supposed to have haunted the third floor of the building where they met their untimely demise. In the rooms of the third floor, boxes flew through the air without any physical explanation. In the room where the murders allegedly occurred, the atmosphere was so oppressively thick and murky, that staff had difficulty breathing. Eventually staff refused to enter the room.

Renovations and Contemporary Times

When the building was renovated to make room for the restaurant's cathedral ceilings, the third floor was removed. Underground tunnels were also discovered with old bottles strewn about. It is suspected that the tunnels were used to smuggle liquor into the tavern during the prohibition era.

During the renovations, strange events occurred. Lights turned on and off for no reason, music played without cause, doors opened and slammed shut of their own volition. Unusual incidents continue to occur at the restaurant.

The strangest story from the history of this unique location occurred during relatively contemporary times. In October of 1982, a woman was discovered deceased in the restaurant's restroom. The official account is that the woman "slipped and cut her throat on the ragged edge of a soap dish."

Some think that this accident was a little too unusual, and perhaps she decided to take her own life in the restaurant's restroom. The world will never know what happened in that restroom on that fateful day. The only witness passed away before her final statement could be recorded for posterity.

D. S. Shanahan's

D. S. Shanahan's history begins with the building's origins as part of the Kings Park Psychiatric Center.

According to legend, the bar, at one time during its history, served as a brothel and a speakeasy during America's ill-conceived prohibition era, when the production and sale of alcohol was made illegal by federal mandate. This legislation did more to enable the flourishing of organized crime than the legal importation, distribution, buying, and selling of alcohol ever did.

This bar is supposed to be haunted by the ghost of a young woman, who was murdered, while working at the bar, by an irate customer.

Stories circulate about the waitress who never clocked out. One employee claims he witnessed a woman wandering the upstairs hallway. When he approached her, calling out to her, wondering why she was wandering, she disappeared into thin air. Tales of the phantom waitress have also been reported by many of the bar's regular customers.

The bar seems to be a popular location not only for the spirit it sells, but also for the spirits of the departed. The lingering presence of a child is also reported to have been seen, not just at, but also underneath the bar, peering out from its shadowed recesses, startling unsuspecting patrons. The ghostly child, according to legend, is the brothel madam's child, also killed in retaliation by an unhappy customer.

It seems that being employed in a bootlegger's brothel was a business whose risk far exceeded its rewards.

Inside the Tree...

In an unrelated legend, an old tree located behind the bar has an interesting shape that has inspired a couple stories of its own. It is said that the way the branches and trunk are arrayed, one can see the shape of a woman trapped inside the tree. Some suggest that the shape is the petrified form of a dryad, a mythical creature that lives inside a tree to protect it from harm. It is said that a dryad is the soul of a tree, and that if a tree's "spirit" dies, the tree will also die. Contrastingly, some argue that the interesting outline is that of an old man with a beard, but maybe the manifestation one sees in the tree depends upon the beholder, functioning much like Rorschach inkblot tests, revealing more about the psyche of the observer than the object being observed.

When all of the many possibilities are weighed with a sober view, perhaps the many legends surrounding this unique location are just examples of the consumption of alcoholic spirits resulting in the viewing of supernatural spirits.

The Phantom Runner of Centerreach High School Track

On the fateful day of January 3, 1997, James Halverson, an off duty F. D. N. Y. firefighter was shot while running on the athletic track used by Centerreach High School, which was near his home.

The story most commonly alleges that William Sodders, a twenty-one-year-old with an obsession for re-enacting violent movie scenes, had been hiding in the woods, watching Halverson running for exercise. Sodders stepped into Halverson's path, pretending to tie his shoe, then stood up abruptly and shot Halverson point blank in the chest. Halverson was left to die from his injury, and in a macabre twist, was reportedly found dead by his pregnant wife sprawled on the high school track. James Halverson was only thirty years old.

The legend, like most contemporary urban folklore has changed some in its retelling, one account maintaining that it was a group of local youths who had come to the track, bored, with a loaded handgun and nothing else to do. Or that a couple of local kids had a gun and wanted to know what it felt like to shoot someone, so they waited in the woods until the fireman came around the northeast corner of the track, they shot him. In this version, both boys were arrested and convicted for killing the firefighter.

Not long after the firefighter's untimely demise, people began witnessing supernatural sights in the northeast corner of Lane 5, where the murder occurred. Some reported seeing a glowing figure, supposedly the supernatural manifestation of the departed firefighter, running along the track late at night. Others have seen the body of a man laying on the track then dissappearing, upon closer observation. Many report the strong sensation of being watched from the south woods where the killer was supposed to have laid in wait, watching his intended victim until he had steeled his nerves enough to commit cold-blooded murder.

According to local legends, the high school's students and visitors for competitive sporting events feel a strong reluctance to sitting on the visitor's bleachers in the northeast corner. Even those who are unaware of the grim history attached to the site don't remain on the south bleachers long before this feeling takes over. Oftentimes, on the north side of the field, the crowd in the stands cheer for the home team, but on the south side of the field, the visiting crowd cheers but they all stand scattered on the field.

Perhaps there's a different kind of school mascot lingering at the school's football field.

Chapter Twelve
Lake View Cemetery

Lake View Cemetery in Patchogue is home to more than one legend.

One of the legends is reflective of Long Island's long history as an integral part of the maritime community that spans the length of America's coast along the Atlantic from Florida to Maine.

The most complete version of the legend seems to center on a ghost named "Whistling Sam." Whistling Sam was a member of the crew of a ship that is rumored to have gone down off Fire Island sometime between 1870 through 1895. Whatever the year, it was winter, and an unkind winter, with record-cold temperatures and torrential storms. A ship called the *Louis V. Place* set sail from Baltimore to New York. Of course, they undertook their journey during an unusually harsh spurt of extremely cold and stormy weather. The weather was so extreme that the ship's sails froze over. This made the ship impossible to maneuver. The crew had been fighting for their lives, against the unforgiving elements without sleep or food or any comforts for days. The ship had been reduced to a glacier, driven mercilessly by the raging fury of the Atlantic, its crew helpless to do anything but ride out the disastrous voyage to its fatal conclusion.

The ship finally succumbed to its fate off the Long Island coast. The residents of the coast of Long Island were no strangers to the misfortune of mariners and their ill-fated vessels. It was common practice for coastal inhabitants to scavenge the wreckage of the many trade ships that floundered off the shores of Long Island.

If the corpses of the crew of the wrecked ships were discovered, they were treated for the most part with due respect and buried in the cemeteries of the coastal communities. This legend is based upon a tale of the rare exception to the hospitality of the coastal people.

In this event, the scavengers brought eight corpses ashore. Seven of the deceased sailors were white. One of them was black. During these days, people had strange and often superstitious beliefs about sailors, especially sailors of African origin. The scavengers presumed that the seven white sailors were Christians and gave them a normal burial in the Lakeview Cemetery located in Patchogue. The scavengers presumed that the black sailor was a non-Christian and buried him in the unhallowed sand of the shore he washed upon.

An insurance company later discovered that the man was the ship's cook, and also a devout Christian. The cook had been affectionately nicknamed "Whistling Sam" by his fellow sailors. Remorsefully, they went to the shore to disinter the body and give the deceased sailor a proper Christian burial. The body was never found.

The body was buried on the shore of Fire Island, and shortly after, his ghost began appearing along the stretch of coastline where he was supposedly interred.

People began reporting the appearance of a very tall black man in a pea coat walking along the beach. Witnesses also heard the forlorn sound of the spirit whistling a winsome melody. The man would mysteriously disappear into the coastal mist when witnesses approached him, attempting to strike up a conversation.

Reports of the whistling spirit dwindled to an end around 1953. A common theory about the ghost's disappearance is that the last of the scavengers who mistakenly buried Sam in the coastal sands may have passed away, allowing Sam to finally find peace.

There is a variation of the tale that also finds its origins in Long Island's maritime history. This version was even published in an article found in the February 28, 1895 edition of the *Brooklyn Eagle*. The basic elements of the tale remain the same, but in this version, the drowned sailors were buried in the Patchogue Cemetery on Blood Hill, adjoining the property of the Patchogue Lace Mill. The young female employees of the mill were afraid to walk home in the evening, and local residents were afraid to go out at night. Their fear was inspired by an eerie nightly phenomenon that began to manifest itself.

An unearthly moaning would begin to emanate from the cemetery at sunset. An ethereal white figure would rise from one of the sailor's graves and would begin wandering about the cemetery, finally settling down at the base of the same nearby tree each night. The apparition would wave and flail about while wailing and disappear as inexplicably as it appeared. The residents theorized that the apparition might have been the manifestation of the restless spirit of one of the deceased sailors.

A further variation contains the accounts of the graveyard ghost, but offers a different explanation for its origin. In this version, the unearthly moaning would begin, then a headless figure would slowly rise from the grave of three sailors who were from the crew of the ill-fated *Louis V. Place*.

The apparition would levitate away from the gravesite, float towards a tree, which was supposedly planted upon the ruins previously occupied by a notorious haunted house. Once the entity reached its nightly destination, it would flail its arms, then fade away, blending into the evening mist.

The house, which had existed there and earned such a notorious reputation, was reportedly owned by an eccentric couple. Renowned author and poet Madame Oakes-Smith shared the home with her husband until 1867. The home lay vacant and gained a ghostly reputation, no doubt in part due to its previous tenants and in part to its location so close in proximity to the graveyard. Literally a "house by the cemetery," the structure eventually, mysteriously, burned to the ground.

Patchogue residents thought that perhaps the silly specter might have been the deceased Mr. Smith, continuing his legacy of eccentricity by visiting his former home from beyond the grave.

Chapter Thirteen
Mount Misery, Sweet Hollow Road, and Mary's Grave,

It seems that Mount Misery, Sweet Hollow Road, and Mary's Grave are the repository of a miscellany of urban legends which are spread by word of mouth as related to the teller of the story by a friend of a friend, or stories told while sitting around campfires or during sleepovers.

The wide variety of supernatural events supposed to inhabit this area give one the impression that if anyone from Long Island were to hear about a ghostly manifestation, and forgot about the location when they shared the story, it was a safe bet to set the story here, making the area an infamous meeting place for paranormal manifestations.

Mount Misery

Mount Misery seems to be an area of Long Island that every Long Islander has heard about, but few people know the exact location occupied by this nexus of paranormal occurrences. It also seems to be inextricably bound with Sweet Hollow Road as a universal location for many of Long Island's urban legends that are not tethered to any specific location. Perhaps the close proximity of a road named Misery, and a road named Hollow, which is a close synonym for Hallow, as in Halloween, presented an irresistible attraction as a destination in which to set ghost stories and urban legends.

According to legend, this region earned its name not from the eerie legends surrounding it, but from its terrain. In the early days of Long Island, this area was not deemed appropriate for use as farmland and became more of a crossroads between farming communities. Because of its hilly landscape, typical of most of New England, and the difficulty horse-drawn wagons had when crossing this terrain, it earned the name of Mount Misery.

Another version of the story is that a mental hospital existed at the crossroads of Mount Misery Road and Sweet Hollow Road. The hospital was supposedly consumed by a raging fire. Only the quick of thought and fast of feet were able to escape, the rest were devoured by the ravaging inferno. Among the lost were all of the hundreds of patients and many of the staff that compassionately stayed behind to try to help their charges escape.

The hospital was supposedly rebuilt fifteen years later, but five short months after the new building opened its doors, it was burned to the ground by an insane woman.

The sound and smell of the twin infernos is said to continue to echo and linger in the woods surrounding the site of this double tragedy. The spirit lights of the incinerated patients are still seen and their cries for help float upon the gentle breezes that wend through the sylvan setting.

A woman in white, commonly called Mary, is also frequently reported as a manifestation around this location.

Stories variously credit the spirit with being the ghost of one of the patients who were trapped in the hospital while it burned or the spirit of the insane arsonist, unable to find rest, wracked by the guilt of her actions, and doomed to roam the area restlessly until the legend of her arsonous deed has faded into obscurity.

There are several varied legends regarding the "Lady in White" which will be explored further in a few paragraphs when we discuss the legends of Sweet Hollow Road.

A different variation on the legend attached to this area is that there was an old style schoolhouse at the crossroads, and that the schoolmaster lost his mind one day and murdered all of his students.

The school was discovered, its floors pooled with the blood of its former students and the teacher was found wandering through the woods. After the mass murder, the teacher was never able to communicate with his fellow man in the manner that he used to and was summarily sentenced to death and executed by hanging for his actions.

His body was buried in the unhallowed ground at the site of the schoolhouse which had been burned down by local townspeople as an unbearable reminder of the atrocity that had taken place.

A further variation on the schoolhouse legend suggests that the schoolhouse simply burned down with all of its students trapped inside.

The Black Dog of Misery

The Black Dog of Misery is said to appear as an unusually large black dog with eyes that shine in the darkness of the forest or glow a demonic red if one is unfortunate enough to see the hellhound at close range. Legends maintain that to see the beast is a harbinger of impending death.

This legend seems more representative of standard American folklore than a unique regional variation. Even in my hometown, it was a common superstition that to see a black dog unaccompanied by a master was a sign that bad luck would soon befall you.

An interesting regional variation suggests that this creature may be more than just a wild dog, and that sometimes the beast walks on two legs and is worshipped in arcane ceremonies by Satanists who live in hidden communes deep in the woods, who communicate by pulling branches of the trees and bending them into coded messages.

The Satanists and their demonic host aren't the only residents rumored to wander the woods of Mount Misery.

There are stories of a mad woodsman who would butcher travelers who journeyed along this remote road. It is rumored that he was never caught, but his spirit continues to roam the woods at night, still wearing his red and black checkered flannel shirt and carrying his well-honed blades, searching for unwary travelers to quench his undying thirst for the blood of the innocent.

Sweet Hollow Road

The sister site of Mount Misery in Long Island Legends is Sweet Hollow Road. Many of the legends attributed to one location are often attributed to either, and the original location of the legends have been blurred through retelling.

Sweet Hallow road is a narrow, twisted, backwoods road surrounded on both side by dense woods. Like many old country roads in the northeast of the United States, the lights along the road are few and far between, which lends the road a surreally evocative and darkly romantic feeling at night.

There is a cemetery visible from the road, which easily lends itself to enhancing the eerie mood of the isolated road and provides fertile ground for the growth of legends.

Many legends have been told and retold about this road. Some are relatively tame. Native American spirits and Revolutionary War era soldiers are reportedly seen through the trees of the densely growing woods either gawking incredulously in awe or running alongside trying to keep pace with the vehicles of voyaging motorists.

Till Death Do We Part…

There are legends of a man or woman seen dressed in unusual clothing walking along the road at night, but if you slow down to see them or stop to offer them a ride, they disappear into the night as if they had never been there.

One legend tells the tale of a newly married couple that had been traveling down the isolated road when they collided with another vehicle, instantly killing the bride and groom. The stories suggest that the ghost may be that of the groom, either eternally searching for his departed bride along the lonesome road, or searching for the reckless motorist who concluded their lives when death did they part.

The ghost may also be that of the bride, searching for her groom. Or it is suggested that she was interred in the cemetery alongside the road, and she walks the road to warn travelers journeying down this darkened path, keeping them awake and aware, lest they meet their maker in a manner reminiscent of hers. Both the bride and groom are rumored to turn and run or jump in front of passing cars if the drivers flash their hi-beams at them. It seems that the ghosts are less than grateful for the warnings of concerned motorists that come much too late.

A less romantic version of the legend concerns a star-crossed couple. The boyfriend was driving. He was also jealous, and in a fit of jealousy, he pushed his girlfriend out of a moving car. The girl survived her unexpected introduction to the asphalt, but was killed by the next car journeying along the roadway.

Other Roadside Tales

The tales of roadside phantoms proliferate in this area. One tale tells of a little girl who was struck by a car while walking along the road in the 1920s. She died from her injuries and her little ghost continues her solitary journey. Another tale tells of two teenage boys who were walking down the road when a car hit them because they didn't hear it coming. The car never warned the boys with its horn. People say that if you don't beep your horn when going under the overpass, the two ghost boys will jump out, trying to frighten you as they seek revenge upon the motorist who struck them down.

A more modern version of this legend is reported to have its origins in the 1970s. A couple of teenagers supposedly formed a suicide pact. Their plan was to hang themselves from the Northern State Parkway overpass, which runs over Sweet Hollow Road. According to local urban legend, they succeeded in their efforts, and if daring motorists honk their horns three times before going underneath the overpass, they will see the supernatural spectacle of the bodies of these two unfortunate suicides.

There was also supposedly a horseback riding camp nearby, where one of the female campers was sexually molested by the counselors. She tried to tell her father, but he wouldn't believe her. Feeling that she was left to defend herself, the girl took bloody revenge, murdering the camp counselors one by one. When she was done with her revenge, the girl hung herself from the overpass. Her ghost is supposed to reappear, swinging where she hung herself on the anniversary of her murder-suicide every year.

A different legend of this area is that if you park under the Northern State overpass and put your car in neutral, it will be pushed back up hill. Also, there are stories of vehicles stalling along the road and unseen hands beating upon the vehicle. When the dead engine is finally revived, there seemed to be nothing wrong with the vehicle that would have caused the car to stall.

Additionally, stories of a phantom car that races down the road at breakneck speeds, eventually seeming to lose control, careening off the road into a flat, marshy section of land. When witnesses pull over to investigate the accident, there's no evidence of the accident ever happening.

One famous tale about the Mount Misery/Sweet Hollow Road area in Huntington, tells of the police officer with half his head missing who stops cars. This phantom cop pulls you over, and everything seems okay until he turns around and the back of his head is missing. Locals believe he pulls people over because he is still looking for his killer.

The Many Legends of Mary

The phantom women in most of the Sweet Hollow stories are called Mary, and the legends are often intertwined with or confused with another popular series of legends popular not only in Long Island, but across New York State and the United States.

The collected folklore of Long Island's many Mary myths integrate elements of several well-known folkloric cycles, among them, Bloody Mary, Black Aggie and La Llorona.

Bloody Mary

Almost everyone in America from Portland, Maine to Portland, Oregon knows the Legend of Bloody Mary, but the particulars of the legendary methods of summoning her vary according to the person telling the tale. Common to all versions is that chanting "Bloody Mary" a predetermined number of times in front of a candlelit mirror will summon a vengeful spirit, although sometimes even the name to be chanted varies.

At least one version recommends slowly spinning while chanting, looking into the mirror after each full turn. The number of chants also varies, usually prescribing an unlucky thirteen. In some accounts, the location of the mirror is unimportant, but most often a bathroom mirror is recommended. In a darkened room, with the lights off, or illuminated solely by candlelight, either a single hand-held candle, or a candle on both sides of the mirror, the daring soul begins the ritual, but what they can expect to occur is a subject of different opinions.

When the apparition has been successfully conjured, she may simply appear and frighten the brave summoner, but the vengeful spirit may not be content with a simple scare and may frighten them intensely enough to drive her visitor beyond the brink of sanity. More extreme accounts claim that

Mary has the power to instantly strike her visitor dead, or to reach through the mirror and scratch her summoner's face off, or drag them back through the mirror to the other side, never to be seen again.

In one Satanic variation, if the brave legend-seeker chants "Hell Mary" seven times in front of a mirror in a dark room, the mirror will run red with blood, and you would see the visage of Satan himself.

"Mirror-witch" tales harken back to the divinational practice of scrying, or staring into a clear or reflective surface with intense concentration to predict the future. These tales are also reminiscent of superstitious supernatural rituals used by girls to divulge what their future husbands would look like.

The uncanny experience of viewing oneself in a reflective surface led to the development of myths of mirrors as portals to other dimensions or planes of existence. These myths are reflected in the tradition of covering the mirrors in a house where a person had recently passed away so that their spirit would not get trapped inside the mirror, rendering the spirit unable to move onto the next intended plane of his existence.

Readers that were paying attention may remember the existence of a blackened mirror of sinister repute from *Chapter Nine* or *The Haunted Mansions and Manors of Long Island*, which was supposed to have had a prominent role in the occult practices of Frank Winfield Woolworth. The Bloody Mary myth was also adapted as the central theme of the popular horror film *Candyman* (1992), directed by Bernard Rose and starring Tony Todd as a unique variation on the myth of the mirror-witch.

Black Aggie

In this well-known legend, and popular story for campfires and sleepovers, a young girl finds herself, at night in a graveyard, at a haunted grave. By some means, her clothes become the means of her accidental tethering to the grave site. This accidental tethering frightens the girl so much that she goes into a panic, and is frightened to death.

The reason for her presence at the grave at this unusual time varies depending on who tells the tale. In many versions, the girl is following through on a bet or a dare to spend the night at a supposedly haunted grave. Interred in the grave is a witch, a warlock, or some other individual of ill repute. It is rumored that anyone staying at the grave overnight on the night of a full moon would be pulled into the grave by the bony hand of the grave's permanent resident, or would be secreted away to the dark side, never to be seen again. Either to prove her presence at the grave, or of her own inspiration, the intrepid young visitor stabs a knife or other sharp implement into the grave, which pins the hem of her loose clothes to the ground. Thinking that the restless spirit has seized her with evil intent, she panics and dies of fright and is either discovered the next day by her friends with a terrified expression on her face, or is never seen again.

In one morbidly romantic version, the girl visiting the gravesite is visiting the final resting place of her young lover, and when her dress gets snagged on a tree-root, she fears that he has reached from beyond the grave to summon her to join him in the afterlife.

An excellent version of this legend is presented in the independent film *Crypt Club* (2004) directed by Miguel Gallego. I had the good fortune to view the film and meet the director during the Rhode Island International Horror Film Festival. He is a uniquely creative individual and I recommend that anyone who enjoys well-made adaptations of urban legends to seek out this short film.

La Llorona

The details of the legend of La Llorona vary depending on the version being told. The common elements are that a woman murders her children, and her spirit is cursed to haunt the place where the murders occurred, frightening the living with her inconsolable cries in the still of the night. Her unearthly wailing is what earned this restless wraith her name "La Llorona" or "the crying woman."

The expanded details of the story vary by version. In many of the versions, the woman becomes involved with a man who is the motivation for the murder of her children. In some versions, a poor woman becomes involved with a man from a higher social station who leaves her and their children to marry a woman from a higher social station. Sometimes the man leaves the woman for another woman to establish a new life, or simply to escape a life of poverty trapped with the woman and her children.

The woman, in the absence of her husband is unable to support her children and takes them down to the river, drowning them to compassionately end their gradual dwindling towards death in the grim grip of poverty.

In a less sympathetic version, the woman murders her children to pursue a relationship with a man who would rather not have children. The man is horrified to discover her murderous deeds, and spurns the woman.

In a reversal of roles recorded in one version, the man is forced to marry the woman when he impregnates her, and after they have more children, he cannot tolerate his family any longer, and takes the children to the river to drown them. The woman dies while trying to prevent her husband's murderous actions, and continues to linger at the site where the multiple murders occurred, mourning her children, and unable to rest until her husband has rejoined her in death.

A moralistic approach suggests that after she commits her heinous deed, she is wracked with guilt, and takes her own life. The woman goes to Heaven and is confronted by the judgement of God. God asks the woman, "Where are your children?" to which she replies, "I do not know." God asks her the question three times and she replies with the same answer, mirroring the threefold denial from the New Testament. God, unsatisfied with her answer, damns the woman to walk the earth, searching for her children for eternity

In southern Mexico, the legend alleges that La Llorona was a prostitute. If she became pregnant, which was a common hazard in her chosen profession, she would abort the children and throw the remains in the nearby river. After having done this for the whole of her career, she died and when she met God to receive her final judgement, God told her she would never be able to enter Heaven until she gathered the spirits of all of the unchristened children she had dispatched. God ordered his angels to dress her in white and send her to find her children.

It is commonly believed that those who hear the cries of La Llorona are marked for misfortune or even death. Those that are brave enough to see La Llorona firsthand provide chilling accounts. In some reports, her eyes are naught but gore-soaked empty sockets. In others, her mouth is extraordinarily large and hosts a mouthful of pointed fang-like teeth, waiting to latch onto her victims so that she can drag them into the river and devour them to provide her with the supernatural strength she needs to continue her unending vigil.

The legend of La Llarona serves as a cautionary tale on several levels. Mexican parents warn their children that bad behavior and being outside after dark will be rewarded with a visit from the vengeful spirit. The tale also serves to caution teenage girls against being enticed by status, wealth, material goods, or by men making declarations of love in the heat of the moment.

Historically, the legend of La Llorona echoes that of the Greek woman Medea, from the Greek play of the same title, who likewise murdered her children after being cast aside for another woman by her husband Jason, of Jason and the Argonauts fame. Medea showed little remorse, instead riding off into the sky on a chariot either pulled by or made of dragons. Also from the tales of Greek Mythology, the Furies, vengeful ghosts who pursue and torment those who commit injustice—especially injustice against women—are a possible thematic precursor to La Llorona.

European folklore also has many similar legends integrating the themes of ethereal women and water. Tales of banshees, female spirits whose wails presage death, may have inspired the legend of La Llorona, and her association with water suggests her ancestors may have been water-nymphs like the Nix, Lorelei, the Sirens, and Melusine.

As previously mentioned, the "Mary's Grave" legend cycle of Long Island integrates elements of all three of these stories as exhibited by the following legends. The Long Island varieties of the legend of Mary's Grave are several and varied, so they are collected by common themes.

Mary's Grave: Mary the Victim

A Young Girl and Her Dog—and Shep Jones

In one version of The Legend of Mary's Grave, Mary and her family had been traveling a long distance in a terrible winter storm. Suffering from the merciless cold, her parents came down with paralyzing cases of pneumonia. Mary left her parents, accompanied by her faithful dog, and sought help at the nearby Jones Estate farm. The Jones followed Mary to where she left her pneumatic parents, but her parents had succumbed to their illness in her absence. The Joneses accepted Mary and her dog, as their own, and Mary worked on the farm to earn her keep, living in a stone shack near the house.

The story would have been a tragic but unmemorable footnote in the history of Long Island, but the suffering of Mary was not to end with the death of her parents. Shep Jones, who seemed to be her benevolent benefactor, was having his way with the farm family's newest addition and threatened to kill her if she dared to tell of his transgressions against her.

In time, Mary could endure no more. When Jones came to use her, she said that she would tell everyone of what had

108

been going on. Jones was furious and attacked Mary, trying to end her life. Mary's faithful and protective companion began barking, in response to which, Jones shot the dog dead and left, thinking that a dead dog was warning enough for young Mary.

Mary was overcome with grief, and wrote a letter detailing the abuse she had been suffering, and hung herself from a tree. The next day, Mrs. Jones discovered the bodies of Mary and her dog and the confessional letter. Outraged and embarrassed, she told the police that Mary had desired Shep, and when Shep turned her down, Mary murdered her dog, and filled with remorse she strung herself up. Mary was supposedly buried unceremoniously on the property, the simple wooden marker for her grave disappearing, subject to the fury of harsh Long Island winters.

Mary's spirit did not rest soundly, and was said to have plagued the prevaricating Jones couple to the end of their days, although they were never officially brought to justice. It is said that Mary's spirit rests unsoundly to this day and that her continued presence continues to manifest itself. Legend claims that Mary's cries can be heard on certain moonless nights, and her spirit may sometimes appear, seeking to keep alive the stories of the injustice inflicted upon her until her name has been cleared of wrongdoing. The angered barking and death cries of her companion are also supposedly heard accompanying the appearance of the spirit of its unfortunate owner.

Mary Was a Child With a Stone Clubhouse

This version of the tale also includes a small house made of stone, and ends with a hanging, but the macabre difference in the stories merit its inclusion.

In this variation on the story, Mary was the daughter of a wealthy man who owned a large area of land that became the home of the town which sprung up around his estate. The man was a solitary type, and built his house away from the town in an isolated part of the property he owned. Living isolated from the townspeople, the girl did not have any friends.

As a gesture of kindness, her father built her a stone clubhouse on the property for her to use as a playhouse. The friendless young girl tried to befriend the animals of the forest and would play with them in her stone clubhouse after gradually earning their trust by overcoming their instinctive fear of humans.

This is where the tale takes a dark turn.

Supposedly, the girl became possessed by a malevolent spirit and murdered her innocent animal friends, mutilating their remains on the stone table within her clubhouse. The girl's possession became complete when she killed her father with an axe.

When the townspeople finally noticed the prolonged absence of the man, they went to his estate to see what had happened. The townspeople found the clubhouse with its collection of mutilated animals and proceeded to the house. They discovered the daughter asleep in her father's bed alongside her father's blood-soaked body. The townspeople roused the girl, desirous of an explanation for their horrifying discoveries. The girl was unable to provide the townspeople with the answers they desired. She had become feral, a wild thing like the animals that had been her friends.

The townspeople, recognized the irrevocable change that had come over the girl. They promptly ended her unfortunate life by hanging her from a tree on the property, and buried her in an unconsecrated, unmarked grave.

The tree remains to this day, by the side of the road. For its role in the events, it looks dead, refusing to bloom since that day. The burn marks from her noose remain on the branch from which she hung.

The house remains atop the hill, and it is said you can see a figure sitting in the window of the master bedroom looking down on the road at curious legend seekers. The stone clubhouse still stands on the road just a bit further up.

Local legends tested the bravery of Long Islanders alleging that if you were brave enough to urinate on Mary's clubhouse, she would appear, but whoever dared, would get into a car crash on their return trip, swerving to avoid hitting a girl in a white dress, supposedly pursuing the trespasser and violator of her childhood haven.

Mary's Grave: Mary the Murderess

In the early days of Long Island, it was primarily rural, dotted with farms which covered wide expanses of the island. A girl named Mary was born of a farming couple. There were complications at the time of her birth, and her mother died from the injuries sustained as a result of these complications shortly after Mary's birth. Mary was an only child, and her father never forgave her for the death of his wife and her mother.

The father, a hateful and lonely man, eventually transgressed the natural boundary between father and daughter and forced an incestuous sexual relationship upon his daughter. The forbidden sexual union, unfortunately, accidentally resulted in Mary's pregnancy. The father, a devout Christian, was torn between the wrong of producing the fruit of an incestuous relationship and the belief that prematurely terminating a pregnancy was against the will of God.

Not knowing what to do, he let Mary carry the child to term, giving birth to his child/grandchild. Mary's father's cruelty did not relent after the birth of her child. In fact, it worsened, inflamed by his horror at being the inadvertent father of a child that was the product of a transgression against the religion he adhered to.

Mary was not invulnerable, and she had finally reached the end of her endurance. In the middle of the night, while her father/lover was asleep, she took her helpless baby to the barn, and mercilessly slaughtered all of the animals in the barn. Mary then climbed to the rafters of the barn and hung her baby, then herself, from coarse hemp rope, ending their miserable lives.

The next day her father/lover, not knowing where she was, went out to the barnyard and discovered the gruesome scene. To save his reputation, he buried Mary and her child in an unmarked grave on his land. Legend claims that if you go to where her graveyard is alleged to be, and you call Mary's name, you can hear the cries of Mary and her child from underneath the unconsecrated grave they share.

A variation on the theme of Mary the murderess suggests that Mary was the victim of domestic violence. Unable to endure the cruelty of her husband anymore she murdered their children in their sleep, then killed herself to rescue them all from a life of pain.

Another variation suggests that Mary was a married woman with many children. Her husband was rumored to be a drunkard, and little help to his wife and children. When she could not deal with the stress of raising her many children by herself, she killed them. When her husband found out about the awful deed, it inflamed his righteous indignation and he was joined by the townspeople in summarily executing Mary for her crime.

The marker of her grave is said to bear the date of her birth, but not her death, suggesting that her soul has been cursed to remain earthbound as punishment for her inexcusable murders. Legend says she continued to haunt the house where she committed the murders, which remained abandoned, gradually sinking into the ground until only the chimney remained visible above ground.

Mary's Grave: The Chandler Estate

Kings Park Psychiatric Center plays a role in this version of the legend.

This version claims that a girl named Mary was discharged from Kings Park Psychiatric Center to live independently on the outside as a tenant of the Chandler Estate.

There are two variations regarding the fate of Mary.

One version claims that Mary disappeared without a trace. Mrs. Chandler discovered her absence when Mary had not been seen for some time and the rent went unpaid. Upon inspecting the suspected abandoned apartment one day, Mrs. Chandler observed that the room still contained all of Mary's meager possessions. Despite Mary's absence, other residents of the Chandler Estate reported hearing noises coming from the room and the lights would inexplicably turn on at night. The room remained empty due to the persistent evidence of an unseen resident, but Mary was never seen again.

A different version suggests that Mary died a horrible and untimely death. Mrs. Chandler, out of pity for her young boarder, and unable to locate Mary's family, had her buried in a cemetery near the boarding house. Legend claimed that if you were perseverant enough to find the grave, and if you flashed your flashlight above the grave on a darkened night, you would see the spirit of Mary appear, mutely appealing her visitors to solve the mystery of her murder.

A Broken Vow, A Hanging Tree, and Maybe a Witch

There are a few variations on the myth of Mary that center themselves around a certain tree of ill repute.

The accounts vary, centering around the theme of relationships which ended badly.

In one account, Mary was accused of being the secret lover of another woman's husband. The rumors, whether or not they were true, caused her to take her own life by hanging herself from a tree. Since suicide is viewed as a mortal sin by Christians, Mary was buried in the unhallowed ground near the tree and continues to haunt the site to this day.

In another account, Mary's boyfriend returned from fighting overseas in one of the world wars. The boyfriend had a lingering suspicion that she had been unfaithful in his absence, and his continuous allegations drove Mary mad. Mary murdered him and then killed herself by hanging at the same tree.

In a third account, Mary's boyfriend discovers that she was unfaithful to him and he went insane with jealousy, dragging her to a remote location and murdered her by hanging her from a tree.

Another story claims that Mary was a nurse who cared for small children. When the children became sick and died from unknown diseases, the parents blamed Mary of witchcraft and killed her, exacting their justice by hanging her from a prominent tree, leaving her body subject to predation to wild animals and a warning to others who would practice witchcraft.

Chapter Fourteen
The Witchcraft Trials of Long Island

Salem, Massachusetts is the most well-known location of witch-trials in America. Although it was indeed an infamous page from early American history, Salem has embraced its notorious reputation for the unfortunate events resulting from rumors, hysteria, and religious intolerance so many years ago. Salem has become a popular gathering place for witches, warlocks, and other individuals interested in witchcraft and the occult. As such a gathering place, Salem is the site of several witch-houses and witch museums open to the public year round.

Salem is also a popular national and international Halloween attraction. Each year thousands of people flock to Salem to celebrate America's most popular unofficially recognized holiday, and many of the city's streets are closed to traffic to accommodate costumed revelers. Although public drunkenness and rowdiness of some participants of the festivities sometimes inspires them to transcend the standards of common public decency, their intoxicated antics are rarely dangerous for the general public and it is truly worth attending if only as another masked face in the crowd.

The events of the Salem witch-trials were also adapted into the dramatic play, The Crucible, by playwright Arthur Miller. The play enjoys an enduring popularity, often selected for presentation by theatrical groups across America, and has been adapted into several movies for the cinema and television. The infamous events are also popular subject matter for television documentaries that take advantage of the seasonal popularity of the paranormal to create new dramatizations of the events each Halloween.

Although Salem is the most famous location of witch-trials in America, Long Island also participated in the prosecution of suspected sorcerers and practitioners of the occult.

Deaths in the Wood family and the Witchcraft Trial of the Halls

In 1664, not long after Christmas, George Wood, a Setauket landowner and innkeeper, became sick and succumbed to his illness. His infant son soon followed him to the grave.

Before his untimely death, George Wood had been at odds with a woman named Mary Hall. Mary Hall had also reportedly made many complaints about one of the sons of the Woods, according to a Mrs. Smith, with whom Mary Hall had also had a few unkind words.

As a result of rumors circulating about the bad blood between the Woods and the Halls, Mary Hall and her husband Ralph were indicted on charges of witchcraft and sorcery in connection with the sudden death of the Woods. The following is an excerpt from the court records of New York City:

"Ralph Hall thou standest here indicted, for that having not the feare of God before thine eyes, Thou did'st upon the 25th day of December, being Christmas day last was 12 Moneths, and at sev'all other times since, as is suspected, by some wicked and detestable Arts, commonly called witchcraft and Sorcery, maliciously and feloniously practice and Exercise, upon the Bodyes of George Wood, and an Infant Childe of Ann Rogers, by which said Arts, the said George Wood and the Infant Childe most dangerously and mortally fell sick, and languisht unto death. Ralph Hall, what dost thou say for thyselle, art thou guilty, or not guilty?"

The Halls pled not guilty, and no public testimony was ever taken. The jury had some questions about the conduct and reputation of Mary Hall, but none about Ralph Hall. They were both found innocent of practicing witchcraft.

The majority of the damaging depositions had come from a Mrs. Smith. The Halls, feeling justly indignant of the charges levied against them, filed a counter-suit. The town records state,

> "The magistrates having Considered the Complaints of Hall and his wife against Mr. Smith, do judge the said of Mr. Smith hath not sufficiently made good what he hath said of her, and therefore Mr. Smith is ordered to pay the woman five markes."

In an ironic turn of events, Richard Smith, the husband of the main accuser of the Halls, had experienced imprisonment and Banishment for Quakerism or Quakerly behavior, but became a man of note after establishing himself in his new home.

The Death of Elizabeth Gardner and the Witchcraft Trial of Goody Garlick

In 1657, in early February, in the small, isolated village of East Hampton, Elizabeth Gardiner Howell, then only sixteen, went to bed with what seemed to be the flu. The young woman's condition worsened and she became delirious, suffering from an uncontrollable fever.

On Saturday, the young woman's mother, Mary, who was ill herself, left her bed to visit her daughter. The young woman reached out to her mother from the haze of her illness and cried out, "Oh, mother, mother, I am bewitched." The young woman also screamed out in her delirium and pointed to the end of her bed where she claimed she saw, "Goody Garlick in the further corner and a black thing at the hither corner, both at the feet of the bed." She further cried, "A witch! A witch! Now you are come to torture me because I spoke two or three words against you!" She was violently flailing her arms out to strike out at what she imagined she saw.

On this same night, Elizabeth told Goody Simons, a neighbor who was staying there, that Goody Garlick, "is a double-tongued woman. Did you not see her last night stand by the bedside ready to pull me in pieces? And she pricked me with pins."

By Sunday evening, young Gardiner Elizabeth Howell was dead.

The death of the young girl did not go unnoticed in the small rural community, nor did the young woman's delirious ravings during her brief and fatal illness.

The rumors of witchcraft spread quickly through the village and soon people started pointing fingers. Most of them pointed to "Goodwife" or "Goody" Garlick, a woman in her 50s, the wife of Joshua Garlick, who had worked on Gardiner's Island.

Goody Garlick's actual name was Elizabeth Garlick. Goodman and Goodwife were not names, but terms of address for married persons.

Soon other women began accusing Goody Garlick of killing their young children. A woman named Goody Davis claimed that, "When I took the child from Goody Garlick, I saw death in the face of it!" and "The child lay five days and five nights and never opened the eyes nor cried till it died."

These allegations became impossible to ignore, and Goody Garlick was brought before the Town Court on Suspicion of Witchcraft. The justices John Mulford, John Hand, and Thomas Baker, held three weeks of hearings, where depositions were taken from thirteen witnesses.

A number of residents told the justices stories about Goody Garlick which hurt her case. All the direct quotations

118

used in this account are copied verbatim from these depositions, which are in the Town of East Hampton archives. Goody Edwards said that once Goody Garlick had requested that Edwards' daughter, who had recently given birth, provide her with some breast milk. The child immediately became sick. Edwards later told this story to Goody Davis, the wife of Foulk Davis, who replied that Goody Garlick had once made the same request of her own daughter, whose child quickly died.

Richard Stratton said that, years earlier, he heard Goody Davis say that her own child died strangely at the Island. "She thought it was bewitched and she said she did not know of any one on the Island that could do it unless it were Goody Garlick."

Goody Birdsall heard the same Goody Davis say that she had dressed her child in clean linen and, "Goody Garlick came in and said how pretty the child doth look. And so soon as she had spoken Goody Garlick said the child is not well for it groaneth and Goody Davis said her heart did rise and Goody Davis said when she took the child from Goody Garlick she said she saw death in the face of it. And her child sickened presently upon it and lay five days and five nights and never opened the eyes nor cried till it died."

One person who did not testify, was Goody Davis, although she is mentioned in almost every other accusation against Goody Garlick. As the testimony continued, it became increasingly apparent that it was this same Goody Davis who seemed to be Goody Garlick's chief accuser. Through the testimony of others, Goody Davis accused Goody Garlick of having caused a miscellany of unexplained happenings on the island, among them, a child that was, "taken away in a strange manner," a man that was dead, a fat and lusty sow, and her piglets that died during the birth, and an ox with a broken leg.

While Lion Gardiner himself did not testify directly, his word carried weight. Gardiner said that another woman working for him had accused Goody Garlick of causing the death of her child. According to Lion Gardiner, Goody Garlick, had taken an Indian Child to nurse, and starved her own child to death for the sake of the pay she was to receive for nursing the Indian child.

After hearing the testimony, and not being skilled in the science of Demonology, the town justices sent her trial to the General Court of Connecticut, in which the occult Doctrine would be applied with greater expertise. Easthampton was then within the Jurisdiction of the Colony of Connecticut.

The indictment was as follows,

> "Thou art indicted by the name of Elizabeth Garlick the wife of Joshua Garlick of East Hampton, that not having the fear of God before thine eyes thou has entertained familiarity with Satan the great enemy of God & mankind & by his help since the year 1650 hath done works above the course of nature to the loss of lives of several persons (with several other sorceries) & in particular the wife of Arthur Howell of East Hampton, for which both according to the laws of God & the established law of this commonwealth thou deservest to die."

The trial was held on May 5, in the Particular Court of Connecticut, with a panel of magistrates headed by the governor, John Winthrop. The trial itself was anticlimactic.

The jury found Goody Garlick not guilty, determining that there was not enough evidence to convict Goody Garlick of the charges levied against her.

Although Elizabeth Garlick was found innocent of the charges against her, her husband Joshua Garlick thought that irreparable damage had been done to the reputation of himself and his wife, and on his wife's behalf, he issued a defamation suit against Goody Davis since it was evident that it was Goody Davis who blamed Goody Garlick for a variety of unexplained events and personal hardships through the testimony of others.

There are no records indicating that the defamation suit ever went to trial.

Elizabeth Garlick and her husband seemed to have lived out the remainder of their lives in East Hampton peaceably enough, living well into their nineties. Their chief nemesis, Goody Davis, appears to have died soon after the trial.

It seems that even if Elizabeth Garlick was not a practitioner of the dark arts, false accusations and unsubstantiated rumors are not viewed favorably by the fickle hand of fate.

In Conclusion

If you have reached the end of this book, I hope that you enjoyed the journey.

I enjoyed my exploration of the folklore and paranormal events of Long Island and I hope I was able to share some of the thrill of exploration and discovery with you.

I thought that writing a book would be much easier than it became.

It became even more difficult when I located resources to assist me with my investigations.

One might think that more resources would make a researcher's investigations easier, but as an author trying to present an original perspective on a folklore so frequently adapted into book form, one must take great pains to avoid plagiarizing the sources that one references.

To insure the rights of the authors whose works I gratefully received for reference and review, I adopted a policy that I would not include any legends referenced to in their works unless I found several additional references to the same legends in other sources and was able to integrate information from a miscellany of sources.

Any stories which I was unable to find additional references to I left untouched out of respect for the original authors initiative and creativity.

It is for this reason that I wholeheartedly recommend any and all of the books mentioned in the "References and Bibliography" section which follows.

You will be pleased to discover many delightfully chilling tales which were not included in this collection, and interestingly unique approaches to the legends contained herein.

Without the work of my predecessors, this book would not exist, and I am grateful for their efforts and generosity and pleased to refer readers towards the preceding body of work.

For that matter, if any readers feel that this book ended too quickly, you can further quench your desire for my writing by visiting the website for Keriann Flanagan Brosky's book, *Ghosts of Long Island: Stories of the Paranormal* (Maple Hill Press, 2006), which also contains a glowing review of that delightful book by your faithful author.

I am also a regular featured contributor to *SCARS* Magazine, and can be contacted through the magazine and will reply to any correspondence as time permits.

References and Bibliography:

Many of the legends of Long Island have become so common that they have assumed a part of the informal public history of Long Island.

As such, a miscellany of different variations are easily accessible through any number of different methods of investigation.

These books were valuable resources suggesting selections from the larger realm of Long Island's paranormal history and folklore.

The author of this book has taken great pains to avoid directly infringing upon original material produced by the authors of the following books.

Print resources

[Otherwise known as books, magazines and newspapers]

These resources were used for the purpose of researching this book.

Flanagan Brosky, Keriann: *Huntington's Hidden Past* (Maple Hill Press, 1995); *Ghosts of Long Island: Stories of the Paranormal* (Maple Hill Press, 2006)

Macken, Lynda Lee: *Haunted Long Island* (Black Cat Press, 2005)

Marcello, Leon: *Creepy Crawls: A Horror Fiend's Travel Guide* (Santa Monica Press, 2006)

Randall, Monica: *The Mansions of Long Island's Gold Coast* (Hastings House Publishers, 1979); *Winfield, Living in the Shadow of the Woolworths* (St. Martin's Press, 2003)

Schmidt, Therese Lanigan: *Ghostly Beacons, Haunted Lighthouses of America* (Schiffer Publishing, Ltd., 2000)

Online Resources

Long Island Oddities: http://www.lioddities.com/index.html. [An excellent website about haunted happenings on Long Island.]

Internet Movie Database: http://www.imdb.com.

SCARS Magazine: www.scarsmagazine.com

[**Disclaimer:** Like the ghostly phenomenon presented in the preceding, these sites may appear for only a limited time on this plane before evaporating into the aether from which they were first fabricated.]